Cambridge Elements ☰

Elements in Criminology
edited by
David Weisburd
George Mason University, Virginia
Hebrew University of Jerusalem

PARTNERSHIPS IN POLICING

How Third Parties Help Police to Reduce Crime and Disorder

Lorraine Mazerolle
University of Queensland

Kevin Petersen
University of North Carolina at Charlotte

Michelle Sydes
Griffith University

Janet Ransley
Griffith University

CAMBRIDGE
UNIVERSITY PRESS

Shaftesbury Road, Cambridge CB2 8EA, United Kingdom

One Liberty Plaza, 20th Floor, New York, NY 10006, USA

477 Williamstown Road, Port Melbourne, VIC 3207, Australia

314–321, 3rd Floor, Plot 3, Splendor Forum, Jasola District Centre,
New Delhi – 110025, India

103 Penang Road, #05–06/07, Visioncrest Commercial, Singapore 238467

Cambridge University Press is part of Cambridge University Press & Assessment,
a department of the University of Cambridge.

We share the University's mission to contribute to society through the pursuit of
education, learning and research at the highest international levels of excellence.

www.cambridge.org
Information on this title: www.cambridge.org/9781009472036

DOI: 10.1017/9781009472029

First published 2024

A catalogue record for this publication is available from the British Library

ISBN 978-1-009-47203-6 Hardback
ISBN 978-1-009-47198-5 Paperback
ISSN 2633-3341 (online)
ISSN 2633-3333 (print)

Additional resources for this publication at www.cambridge.org/Mazerolle

Partnerships in Policing

How Third Parties Help Police to Reduce Crime and Disorder

Elements in Criminology

DOI: 10.1017/9781009472029
First published online: December 2024

Lorraine Mazerolle
University of Queensland

Kevin Petersen
University of North Carolina at Charlotte

Michelle Sydes
Griffith University

Janet Ransley
Griffith University

Author for correspondence: Lorraine Mazerolle, l.mazerolle@uq.edu.au

Abstract: Partnerships in policing are used worldwide to reduce crime and disorder problems. Police forge partnerships with businesses, government agencies, and communities to co-produce public safety. Third-party policing (TPP) is a particular type of partnership that involves the police addressing crime and disorder by working through (and with) third-party partners. This Element focuses on the nature and effectiveness of TPP partnerships. Using systematic review and meta-analytic techniques, it shows that TPP interventions are effective in efforts to reduce crime and disorder, without displacement of these problems. Cooperative partnerships are associated with considerably larger crime control effects than interventions relying on coercive engagement styles. Dyad partnerships – twosome partnerships between police and one third party – are likely to offer the "sweet spot" in TPP. The Element concludes that partnership policing using non–criminal justice legal levers is a promising approach to crime control. This title is also available as Open Access on Cambridge Core.

Keywords: Third-party policing, multi-agency partnerships, cross-sector partnerships, legal levers, systematic review

ISBNs: 9781009472036 (HB), 9781009471985 (PB), 9781009472029 (OC)
ISSNs: 2633-3341 (online), 2633-3333 (print)

Contents

1 Introduction

Third-party policing (TPP) is a particular form of partnership policing that is distinct from the myriad of other forms of partnership policing such as focused deterrence, community policing, problem-oriented policing, and situational crime prevention. Nearly twenty years ago, and reiterated with updated data in this Element, Mazerolle and Ransley (2005) discovered that fewer than a third of TPP interventions occur within the context of a structured program of crime control and that most (at least two-thirds) TPP interventions involve ad hoc, one-off approaches. These ad hoc partnership approaches typically evolve very locally and under the initiative of a single police unit wanting to deal with a specific crime problem on their beat. In this introductory section we situate the emergence of TPP in its historical context, reiterate some of the defining features of TPP, and describe the distinctiveness of TPP from other forms of partnership policing.

1.1 Historical Context

An extensive literature exists that describes shifts from the mid twentieth century onwards in the legal, social, economic, and governance frameworks affecting policing (see Bayley, 2016; Brodeur, [2008] 2014; Garland, 2002; Mazerolle & Ransley, 2005; Mazerolle et al., 2019; O'Malley, 2000; Ransley & Mazerolle, 2009; Wood & Shearing, 2006). These shifts included changes in police focus from being predominantly reactive to preventive, focusing on crime prevention and proactive policing (Crawford & Evans, 2017; Weisburd & Majmundar, 2018; Zedner & Ashworth, 2019). The shifts in frameworks have also involved an increasing concern with risky individuals, groups, places, and practices as potential crime generators (Eck, 2019; Ericson & Haggerty, 1997). Cumulatively, the rise of the new regulatory state (Braithwaite, 2000; Scott, 2000) has led to new regulatory domains and bodies with enforcement responsibilities and powers.

One outcome of these shifting frameworks has been increasing pressure on police to form partnerships, networks, webs, and nodes focused on community safety, security, and crime prevention (Ayling & Grabosky, 2006; Bayley & Shearing, 2001; Brodeur, [2008] 2014). Many police, institutional, and governance frameworks now embed the formation of partnerships as a key strategy and performance measure (Fleming, 2006; Mazerolle, 2014; van Felius et al., 2023) and, in some cases, a legislated requirement (Crawford & Evans, 2017; Mazerolle et al., 2012).

A common strategy is for police to partner with regulators (Mazerolle & Ransley, 2019; Scott, 2018) in multiagency partnerships (Andrews, 2023) with police turning to partners who can give "assistance in altering the causes and conditions driving the problem … [where] not uncommonly those others are government regulators" (Scott, 2018, p. 87). Such partnerships aim to promote joined-up responses to complex problems often involving the same populations or places (Mazerolle, 2014; Meyer & Mazerolle, 2014). For police, partnerships bring access to additional resources (Ayling, 2013; Thacher, 2022) and to the legal powers held by other agencies. The harnessing of these legal powers for crime control purposes constitutes the foundation of TPP.

Multiagency and multi-nodal partnerships in policing pose many parallel challenges to those identified in the amorphous literature on cross-sector partnerships (Clarke & Crane, 2018; van Tulder & Keen, 2018; van Tulder et al., 2016). For example, drawing from broad transdisciplinary research, Seitanidi and Crane (2014) find that cross-sector partnerships are often adopted by organizations to tackle intractable problems using novel solutions. Le Ber and Branzei (2010) find that cross-sector partnerships can increase the efficiency and effectiveness of dealing with a myriad of problems. In crime control, cross-sector partnerships can bolster resources and expertise, and broaden available tactics beyond those held by police.

1.2 Defining Features

The key defining feature of TPP is that police indirectly, rather than directly, target crime and disorder problems, and they do so through a partnership with a third party and through the legal levers available to that third party (see Mazerolle, 2014; Mazerolle et al., 2016). In TPP, the police carefully harness a third-party partner's legal lever(s) to tackle crime problems (Buerger & Mazerolle, 1998). In essence, TPP comprises three component parts: (1) public police (being the "first party"), (2) the person, place, or situation at the center of the crime or disorder problem being targeted (being the "second party"), and (3) an external entity (being the "third party") that the police partner with to control or prevent the crime or disorder problem.

In TPP, the "first party" is defined as the public police who work in partnership with a third party for the purpose of controlling or preventing a crime and/ or disorder problem. Partnerships may be forged in an episodic manner (see Mazerolle & Ransley, 2005), through a program of crime control activities (e.g., focused deterrence, on which see Braga & Weisburd, 2012), or because the partnership is mandated by law (e.g., UK Crime and Disorder Act 1998; Scottish Police and Fire Reform Act 2012).

The "second party" in TPP is defined as the ultimate crime control or prevention target (see Buerger & Mazerolle, 1998; Mazerolle & Ransley,

2005). "The ultimate target of a TPP intervention can be a problem person (a motivated offender), a problem place (an amenable place), or a problem situation (a suitable target, absence of suitable controllers) (see Cohen & Felson, 1979; Eck, 1994; Felson, 1995)" (Mazerolle et al., 2016, p. 4).

The "third party" is central to the TPP approach. A third party is an entity – a person, agency, organization, or business – operating within a legal framework and with legal powers and responsibilities not directly available to police. The third party is valuable to police because they have access to at least one non–criminal justice legal lever that is (or could be) applied to control or prevent a crime or disorder problem (see Mazerolle et al., 2016). The third party (or third parties) partners with police and is the key agent of crime control within TPP. A third party can be an individual (e.g., a bar staff member, a property owner), an organization (e.g., the Pharmacy Guild), a business (e.g., a bar), a regulatory authority (e.g., a liquor licensing authority, a local council), a government department (e.g., an education department), or a network of collaborating agencies (e.g., see Green, 1996). Most often, though, as shown in the studies included in our analysis, third parties are regulatory authorities who hold not only relevant legal levers but also a shared interest in the problem, even if that interest arises under a different framework. For example, a local authority may be interested in the health and safety problems caused by how slum landlords manage particular properties, whereas police are interested in those same properties because of the crime and disorder problems they generate.

1.3 Distinctiveness from Other Forms of Partnership Policing

Partnerships in policing are not new. Early co-production of crime control involved a range of different types of partnership between police and citizens (see, e.g., Ostrom & Ostrom, 1979; Ostrom et al., 1978). The most recent surge in partnership approaches in policing emerged from failures in the standard, reactive model of policing (Goldstein, 1979) and global transformations in governance and regulation from the 1990s (see Mazerolle & Ransley, 2005 for review) that brought about a host of plural, networked styles of policing (Loader, 2000). In the rest of this section we explore the ways in which TPP partnerships are similar, but most importantly how TPP is different and distinct from other forms of partnerships in policing.

1.3.1 Community Policing

Community policing – or community-oriented policing – emphasizes the central role of policing partnering with communities to co-produce public safety. Community policing involves a series of broad-ranging approaches to crime control and is generally described as having three components: partnerships, organizational reform, and a focus on problem-solving (see Gill et al., 2014; Oliver, 1998; Skogan, 2009). Community policing initiatives seek to influence a number of key outcomes such as increases in police legitimacy and citizen satisfaction along with decreases in fear of crime and local crime rates. The types of intervention deployed by police in community policing include foot patrols, community newsletters, community meetings, citizen-police academies, door-to-door visits (including surveys), education programs in schools, neighborhood watch, weekend graffiti cleanups, and participation in multiagency partnerships (see Mastrofski et al., 1995; Skogan, 2007; Weisburd & Eck, 2004).

The partnerships referred to in most of the community policing literature are typically geographically bounded engagements with local citizen groups. The partners include church or faith-based organizations, neighborhood watch groups, block clubs, community councils, school-based parent groups, sporting organizations, community consultative committees, and local merchant associations. These partnerships comprise several key characteristics: enlisting the help of citizens to deal with local crime problems (see Skogan, 2009), giving a voice (or collective voice) to citizens in setting police priorities to deal with local crime problems (see Bayley, 1994), being a vehicle for police to gather community intelligence about crime problems (see Bullock, 2013; Innes & Roberts, 2007), helping police to communicate accurate information about the specifics of local crime problems to dispel myths and reduce fear (see Bennett, 1991; Weisburd & Eck, 2004), and educating citizens around the rationale for policing strategies and priorities (see Somerville, 2009).

The priority partnerships in TPP are fundamentally different from those fostered in community policing. The key partners in TPP are those entities that possess a specific legal lever. The community groups and entities that are the foundation of community policing partnerships rarely, if ever, possess a legal provision. To be sure, in some TPP interventions – many included in this review – the multiagency interventions include both partners with legal levers and those without legal levers (see Section 4). Yet, as we will show in Section 5, the critical element in the effectiveness of TPP partnerships is the presence of those entities that possess and use their legal levers. We hasten to add that this does not mean that the police should discount their engagement with community groups in their community policing efforts to reduce crime and fear of crime and improve citizen satisfaction and trust in the police. Indeed, Gill and colleagues' (2014) systematic review of community policing shows that, while community-oriented policing strategies have limited effects on crime and fear of crime, the strategy has positive effects on citizen satisfaction, perceptions of disorder, and police legitimacy. Citizen engagement may play an important role in TPP but it is the involvement of third-party partners with a legal provision that bolsters the capacity of the police to be effective in their efforts to reduce crime.

1.3.2 Situational Crime Prevention

Situational crime prevention (SCP) seeks to prevent crime by reducing opportunities (Clarke, 2009). Many – but not all – of the twenty-five techniques included in SCP (Cornish & Clarke, 2003) involve partnerships between police and other entities. The wide range of techniques available in SCP include organizational, physical, and situational approaches that increase the effort and risks – and reduce the rewards, provocations, and excuses – associated with the commission of a crime (Clarke, 2009). Police partnerships in SCP are effective in combating many forms of crime, such as robberies and vehicle crimes (Farrington & Welsh, 2009; Welsh & Farrington, 2008), wildlife crimes (Moreto & Gau, 2017; Pires & Clarke, 2012), terrorism (Clarke & Newman, 2007), and cybercrimes (Ho et al., 2022).

The conceptual synergies between SCP and problem-oriented policing (POP; see Section 1.3.3) pertaining to the crime triangle (Eck, 2003) provide an opportunity to explore how the partnerships in SCP interventions (and POP interventions) might be generated in different and distinct ways relative to how partnerships are forged in the context of TPP interventions. Using the crime triangle model (also known as the problem analysis triangle) (Eck, 2003), the types of partnership in SCP fall into three categories: a partner who is a guardian of a target or victim, a partner who is a place manager of a criminogenic place, and/or a partner who serves as a handler for a motivated offender. A guardian partner is generally an ordinary citizen whose presence discourages crime from occurring, such as homeowners taking crime prevention responsibility for their homes (Reynald, 2016; Zahnow & Corcoran, 2022). A place manager as a policing partner is someone (or a group of people or an entity) who has some level of responsibility over a problem place, such as employees in a bar that is prone to fights (see Madensen, 2007). A handler as a policing partner is generally described as a prosocial adult – like a parent – who has some level of control over a young person's behavior (see Tillyer & Eck, 2011). The partners who possess specific legal levers in SCP interventions are generally those who are place managers. This geographic focus of place manager partnerships in policing, where the place manager possesses and uses a legal lever in their efforts to control crime, is a clear point of similarity among SCP, POP, and TPP interventions. However, the SCP (and POP) partnerships with handlers and guardians do not generally meet the criteria of a TPP partnership approach to crime control given their lack of access to a specific legal lever.

One recent contribution to the theory and practice of SCP and POP is the concept of "super controllers" (see Sampson et al., 2010) that offers some important synergies with TPP. Super controllers are the "people, organizations and institutions that create the incentives for controllers [managers, guardians and handlers] to prevent or facilitate crime" (Sampson et al., 2010, p. 40). Sampson and colleagues (2010) go on to describe the range of super controllers as being formal (such as the courts, regulatory agencies, financial institutions), diffuse (such as markets that regulate behavior, media, and political decisions), and personal (such as groups and family). There are clear synergies between TPP partners and the formal category of super controller, where the incentives for control are based in some type of legal provision. For example, Sampson and colleagues (2010) describe organizational rules and procedures, contractual conditions, and regulatory laws that are administered by health agencies, fire departments, and a host of other entities. Through this lens, the necessary condition of TPP being a partner with a legal lever can be viewed as engaging explicitly with a super controller.

1.3.3 Problem-Oriented Policing

One of the most widely adopted approaches to crime prevention, POP requires the police to be proactive in identifying and addressing underlying patterns that generate recurring crime and disorder problems (see Goldstein, 1979; Hinkle et al., 2020; Weisburd & Eck, 2004). From the outset, Goldstein (1979) called for police to draw upon civil statutes and regulatory provisions alongside community resources and criminal laws to tackle recurring problems. The underlying assumption of POP, therefore, is that "successful implementations of POP would be reliant on forming partnerships with other agencies, community organizations and community members to deliver non-law enforcement responses" (Hinkle et al., 2020, p. 3). These partnerships that involve "other agencies" are where TPP and POP have overlap. Yet, despite this overlap, the processes for identifying and working with these "other agency" partners differ between POP and TPP interventions.

The POP model of approach is the subject of enormous attention in the extant literature, with the creation in 2002 of the POP Center, which now contains a vast library of case studies and resources.[1] Fundamental to contemporary POP approaches is the SARA (scanning, analysis, response, and assessment) model that prescribes the process the police should use in addressing recurring crime

---

[1] See the POP Center, https://popcenter.asu.edu/

and disorder problems (Eck & Spelman, 1987). The four general prescribed steps in the problem-solving approach include a sixty-step crime analysis manual along with a myriad of other learning support tools to help police as they systematically work through the SARA process. Critical to the POP process is not engaging with a response or forging a crime control partnership with an outside agency without first scanning for a recurring issue and conducting an in-depth analysis of the problem scope, nature, and causes (see Braga, 2008). The scanning and analysis steps in POP lead police to a specific partner depending on what the analysis uncovers. The POP approach, as conceptualized by the SARA model, is a clear success story in policing effectiveness: Hinkle and colleagues (2020), in their updated systematic review, reveal strong and consistent evidence that POP is a highly effective approach to reducing crime and disorder.

There are two ways to explore the relationship between POP and TPP: first, TPP can be easily viewed as a subset of POP interventions. However, TPP would include only those POP interventions that involved partners who possessed and used legal levers, as well as those that followed the SARA process, even including those POP interventions that conducted what is known as "shallow" problem-solving (Braga & Weisburd, 2006). In our corpus of TPP interventions included in this review, six out of the twenty-four studies (25 percent) fall within the realm of a POP intervention. By contrast, eighteen of the twenty-four studies (75 percent) in our corpus of TPP interventions are not identifiable as a POP project. This ratio of TPP interventions as stand-alone interventions versus being a part of a POP project matches very closely to what Mazerolle and Ransley (2005) found twenty years ago: that fewer than a third of TPP interventions occur within the context of a structured program of crime control. In other words, some TPP interventions are also POP, but far more are not.

In TPP, the partnership with an entity that possesses and uses a legal lever is required to follow the procedures laid out in the law. Regardless of whether the intervention is part of a POP project or not, the steps that need to be taken to apply noncriminal laws are specific (see Section 4). Mazerolle and colleagues (2016) align the legal levers used in TPP interventions to the Braithwaite (2006, 2011) regulatory pyramid framework showing that the codified processes for regulating conduct, inducing cooperation, and incentivizing prosocial behavior are undertaken in a series of sequential steps, often with time delays between each step to give the target of control (a delinquent person, situation, or place) the opportunity to conform and avoid escalating action. The focus on these regulatory steps, the time delays between steps, and the legal requirements to demonstrate failure to comply do not often align and sit comfortably (particularly temporally) with the SARA steps in the POP process.

1.3.4 Focused Deterrence

Focused deterrence is situated squarely as a strategy that seeks to change offender behavior by increasing the risks of apprehension faced by offenders and using a range of methods to directly communicate to targeted offenders very clear incentives to comply and disincentives to offend (see Braga & Weisburd, 2012). Often using the SARA processes of POP, the targets of focused deterrence strategies are offenders or groups of offenders. Braga and Weisburd (2012) add, however, that while the emphasis of focused deterrence is on increasing the risks for targeted offenders, the approach also involves "decreasing opportunity structures for violence, deflecting offenders away from crime, increasing the collective efficacy of communities and increasing the legitimacy of police actions" (p. 26). These varied mechanisms of change in focused deterrence contrast to the more narrowly conceived mechanism of change that is described by Mazerolle and colleagues (2016), who argue that the harnessing of legal levers prioritizes, legitimizes, and structures the partnerships between police and third parties, thereby increasing the application of legal levers in a more consistent and reliable manner which motivates targets to comply with the law being applied.

In focused deterrence, the police convene interagency working groups that comprise a range of law enforcement and criminal justice agencies that have a stake in the crime problem (including police, school police, probation, parole, state and federal prosecutors, and sometimes federal enforcement agencies) along with social service providers and community-based practitioners (Braga & Weisburd, 2012). Kennedy (1997) explains that other agencies such as the Bureau of Alcohol, Tobacco, Firearms and Explosives as well as federal and district attorneys also comprise part of the interagency working group. The partnerships in focused deterrence, therefore, are characterized as multiagency interventions using forums with the offenders and gang members to communicate clear messages to the offenders (Braga, 2008). By contrast, the focus of TPP partnerships is much more narrowly focused on non–criminal justice agencies that possess and use a specific legal lever. We expand on how limiting the number of partners in a TPP intervention contributes to the effectiveness of the strategy in Section 5.

The "pulling levers" component of focused deterrence strategies involves a "varied menu of sanctions" (Braga & Weisburd, 2012, p. 8). These levers include "serving warrants, mounting federal prosecutions, changing the conditions of community supervision for probationers and parolees" (Braga et al., 2019b, p. 229). Kennedy (1997) adds that restraining orders, bail conditions, reopening old cases, and seizing weapons and assets can be part of the menu of sanctions. Focused deterrence levers, therefore, tend to draw from criminal law provisions, whereas TPP explicitly draws on non–criminal justice legal levers (see Section 5). Further, TPP interventions typically use civil laws, and the civil standard of proof, while focused deterrence relies primarily – but not exclusively – on enforcement of the criminal law. Hence, focused deterrence is usually activated where there is a high degree of evidence of criminal behavior, whereas TPP can be activated in a more preventive and disruptive way, to break up gangs, for example, where individual criminality may be hard to prove. One type of TPP intervention bears some similarity to focused deterrence: TPP involving civil orders against individuals, such as gang or drug house injunctions (discussed in Section 4), often target similar kinds of problem places, people, or gangs to those targeted in focused deterrence.

In summary, the key points of difference between focused deterrence and TPP are that (1) focused deterrence partnerships tend to be complex, multiagency partnerships, whereas TPP interventions are often concentrated on just one partner working actively with police (see Section 5); (2) legal levers in focused deterrence are primarily criminal justice levers, whereas TPP levers are defined specifically as non–criminal justice levers; and (3) the key mechanism of change in focused deterrence is offender notification meetings that stress individual deterrence, normative change in offender behavior, and increasing views on legitimacy and procedural justice. In contrast, the mechanism of change in TPP is the police act of harnessing a legal lever to prioritize, legitimize, and structure the partnership, thereby increasing the application of a non–criminal justice legal lever in a more consistent and reliable manner to motivate targets to comply with the law.

1.4 Summary Comments

This section started by providing a brief overview of the historical context in which TPP operates, drawing from a large body of literature on TPP (see in particular Buerger & Mazerolle, 1998; Mazerolle & Ransley, 2005; Mazerolle et al., 2016). It then described the defining features of TPP before turning to an analysis of how TPP is distinctive from other partnership forms of policing, particularly community policing, POP, SCP, as well as focused deterrence. While these partnership-oriented approaches to policing often embody overlapping characteristics, the distinctions offer some important considerations for making practical policy decisions.

The two key defining features of TPP are the formation of a (1) partnership between police and another entity that possesses and activates a (2) non–criminal justice legal provision to control and prevent a crime problem (or problems). In TPP, the availability of a legal lever that is the responsibility of an entity with which the police form a partnership represents the two necessary and sufficient conditions that define and distinguish TPP from other partnership forms of policing. In each TPP intervention there will be an activation process for the legal lever dictated by the relevant regulation. By contrast, in community policing, POP, SCP, and focused deterrence, the partnership is a necessary but not sufficient condition and the legal lever that a partner might possess is neither a necessary nor a sufficient condition to classify the intervention.

Section 2 describes the method and approach we took to conduct a systematic review and meta-analysis of TPP programs used by police since 1980. Section 3 then presents the primary results of the systematic review and meta-analysis, focusing on the question of how effective TPP is in efforts to reduce crime and disorder. Section 4 uses these review data to examine the legal levers used in TPP interventions to ascertain which types of legal lever are associated with effective TPP interventions and which ones are not. Section 5 examines the number of partnerships in the review corpus of TPP interventions to explore the "sweet spot" in terms of the optimal number of partners in successful TPP interventions. Section 6 focuses on comparing and contrasting cooperative and coercive partnerships, highlighting the different types of engagement in TPP that work best to reduce crime and disorder. The Element concludes in Section 7 with a discussion about the theoretical and policy implications of partnership policing in general, and the specific case of TPP.

2 Methods

We conducted a systematic review and meta-analysis to evaluate the effectiveness of TPP interventions. Systematic reviews provide transparent and replicable approaches to "locating, appraising, and synthesizing" (Farrington & Welsh, 2002, p. 9) existing research on a topic, while meta-analysis allows researchers to statistically "summarize the results of empirical studies" (Lipsey & Wilson, 2000, p. 1) identified during a systematic review. Given sufficient conceptual similarity between studies, a systematic review and meta-analysis can provide a more precise understanding of a body of research compared to that offered by narrative interpretations alone. In the context of TPP, our systematic review and meta-analysis draws on Mazerolle and colleagues' (2016, p. 14) protocol to answer the following questions:

(1) What impact does TPP have on crime and disorder?
(2) Does the impact of TPP vary by the target of the intervention (e.g., people vs. places)?

(3) Does the impact of TPP vary by the engagement style of the partnership (cooperative vs. coercive)?

(4) Does the impact of TPP vary by the type of legal lever or third party used?

(5) Does the impact of TPP vary by the type of crime or disorder targeted?

To answer these questions, we synthesized existing evaluation research on TPP interventions that met very specific inclusion requirements (Mazerolle et al., 2016). In this section, we describe these inclusion requirements and the analytical and statistical methods used to synthesize study findings.

2.1 Eligible Interventions, Methods, and Outcomes

All studies included in this review had to meet the four basic criteria. First, eligible studies had to articulate an intervention that involved a partnership between police and at least one third party. A third party is defined here as an entity possessing a specific legal lever which is external to the criminal justice system. These third parties can include individuals (e.g., a bar staff member, a property owner), organizations (e.g., the Pharmacy Guild), businesses (e.g., a bar), regulatory authorities (e.g., liquor licensing authorities, local councils), or government departments (e.g., an education department).

Second, the third-party partner had to activate a non–criminal justice legal lever in the intervention. A legal lever refers to the legal authority or power(s) that an entity is tasked with implementing or enforcing to govern social, economic, or operational activities within a specific jurisdiction. Legal levers encompass a range of measures, including conduct licensing (e.g., alcohol, firearms), mandatory reporting (e.g., chemical sales, child abuse), orders to control behavior (e.g., gang or domestic violence injunctions, truancy regulations), orders under regulatory codes (e.g., building, fire, health and safety, noise codes), and property controls (e.g., drug nuisance abatement) (see Mazerolle et al., 2016).

Third, the intervention evaluation had to measure at least one crime or disorder outcome. We included a range of crime and disorder measures:

(1) official measures of crime (e.g., arrest data, crime rates, calls-for-service data)

(2) unofficial measures of crime (e.g., citizen-reported crime via interview or survey)

(3) displacement of crime and/or disorder (see Telep et al., 2014)

(4) diffusion of crime control benefits

(5) systematic observations of disorder including both social disorder (e.g., public intoxication, loitering, solicitation, excess noise, drug dealing) and

physical disorder (e.g., dilapidated or abandoned properties, rubbish, graffiti)

(6) citizen- or practitioner-reported observations of social or physical disorder (as defined in point [5]).

Fourth, we exclusively focused on quantitative research employing randomized experimental methods (such as randomized controlled trials [RCTs]) or robust quasi-experimental designs (e.g., designs with a control/comparison group). Typically, the control group or comparison condition adhered to standard policing practices, commonly referred to as "business-as-usual." These studies compared outcomes between experimental units implementing a specific TPP intervention and those who continued with routine practices. While less common, we also included comparison groups that received either no intervention or an alternative intervention (known as treatment-treatment designs, see Eck & Wartell, 1998; Payne, 2017; Warpenius & Holmila, 2008). While not as rigorous as RCTs, robust quasi-experiments offer valuable insights into causal relationships when the design is structured to minimize threats to internal validity (Farrington, 2003). To be included in the meta-analysis, evaluations were required to report either a standardized effect size or sufficient data to permit an effect size calculation. We contacted all corresponding authors for additional information for those eligible studies where the data reported were insufficient to compute an effect size and standard error.

2.2 Search Strategy

Our review updates and extends a systematic review and meta-analysis conducted by Mazerolle and Ransley (2005). The earlier review identified seventy-six studies yet, on further screening, only ten studies drawn from 1990 to 2004 (inclusive) met the above four criteria. To update the earlier review we used the corpus of 7,069 eligible policing evaluation studies included in a large-scale policing evaluation database – the Global Policing Database (GPD)[2] – to identify eligible studies from 2005 to 2019. Creation of the GPD started in 2012 with foundation funding from the Australian Research Council, the London Mayor's Office for Policing and Crime (MOPAC), and the College of Policing in the United Kingdom. It is a collaboration between the University of Queensland and Queensland University of Technology, hosted at the University of Queensland. The database is designed to capture all published and unpublished experimental and quasi-experimental evaluations of policing interventions since 1950, with annual harvests conducted to update the database. Studies

---

[2] Access the GDP at https://gpd.uq.edu.au/

held within the GPD are not restricted by outcome measures, language of the research, or type of policing intervention.

The GPD is compiled using systematic search and screening techniques, including a comprehensive systematic search of published and unpublished literature sources. All records are initially screened for relevance to policing based on the title and abstract. If deemed relevant, records then proceed to a staged full-text eligibility screening process to confirm the presence of a quantitative impact evaluation of a policing intervention. The full GPD protocol with details about the search terms and screening methodology can be found on the GPD website.

We used the following keywords in the GPD online search facility to identify potential eligible studies: partner, third-party, multi-agency, civil remedy(ies), regulation, law, legal, lever, collab, code, ordinance, civil order, licensing. The search of the GPD using these keywords returned 2,840 records from 2005 to 2019 that were then screened for inclusion in our review. We screened the 2,840 records for eligibility using the first three criteria identified earlier (see Section 2.1). The search and screening methods used to generate the full GPD corpus of eligible studies satisfied the fourth and final criteria regarding eligible methods included in the review. Of the 2,840 records identified in our keyword search, we identified an additional 14 studies from 2005 to 2019 (inclusive) that met all four of our review criteria.

We also hand-searched specific journals (see table 1 in Mazerolle et al., 2016, p. 18) and conducted reference harvesting of eligible studies and from relevant systematic reviews. We asked experts in the field to review our list of eligible studies, too. No extra studies were identified using these methods.

2.3 Data Extraction and Management

The included studies are listed in the Online Appendix. The following data and information from all included studies were extracted from each included study (see Online Appendix for a summary of the included studies):

(1) a description of the study intervention including the content and delivery
(2) the setting of the intervention
(3) details of all partners in the intervention
(4) the number of partners with and without legal levers
(5) the specific details of the legal levers available
(6) the cooperative versus coercive nature of the intervention
(7) the outcome measures
(8) data to capture all effect size calculations, including sample size

(9)   the research design, including the comparative intervention

(10) the country of the study intervention

(11) the publication type

(12) the target of the intervention, including people or places (micro or macro).

2.4 Measures of Treatment Effect

A fundamental component of meta-analysis is the concept of standardization (Borenstein et al., 2009; Cohen, 1988; Lipsey & Wilson, 2000). As is common with research in social sciences, studies that measure the same conceptual outcome often use very different forms of measurement. For example, measures of crime and disorder may be derived from incident data, calls-for-service data, systematic social observations, or victimization surveys (e.g., see Addington, 2009). The problem this presents for researchers is that of comparability, as a unit change in one form of measurement may not be directly comparable to a unit change in another form of measurement. To solve this, meta-analysis is based on standardized measures of treatment effect, producing values that are "interpretable in a consistent fashion across all the variables and measures involved" (Lipsey & Wilson, 2000, p. 4).

The type of standardized effect size used in a meta-analysis is often dependent on the level of measurement – or the specific form of the data – used to analyze the outcome of interest. In the evaluations of TPP included in this review, crime and disorder was typically measured using ratio-level count data corresponding to geographic areas such as hotels/motels, pharmacies, rental properties, neighborhoods, or entire communities. In place-based studies such as these, crime counts are often reported as rates or averages across varying intervals of time, ranging from weeks to months or years. However, common measures of effect size such as Cohen's d (see Cohen, 1988) are sensitive to the way in which these data are divided across space and time. The same total number of crime incidents occurring within a treatment and control area over a set period can produce considerably different values of Cohen's d if those incidents are divided by weeks versus months or years (see Wilson, 2022). As such, our analyses required an effect size metric capable of handling these differences consistently.

Thus, we used the relative incident rate ratio (RIRR) proposed by Wilson (2022; see also Lum et al., 2020) as the preferred effect size metric for place-based crime prevention studies. The RIRR is a difference-in-difference measure representing the proportional pre- to post-intervention change in crime counts for treatment areas relative to control areas. In contrast to Cohen's d, which provides the estimated treatment effect in standard deviation units, the RIRR provides the estimated treatment effect as a proportional difference in the outcome being counted (i.e., crime). The RIRR is calculated on the natural log scale and can be expressed as follows:

$$\ln(\text{RIRR}) = \ln\left[\frac{(x_{11}/t_{11})(x_{00}/t_{00})}{(x_{01}/t_{01})(x_{10}/t_{10})}\right] \tag{1}$$

Here, subscript one represents the treatment (1) or control (0) group and subscript two represents the post-intervention (1) or pre-intervention (0) period. Accordingly, the x_{ij} terms represent the pre- and post-intervention crime counts for each group, and the t_{ij} terms represent the sample sizes or sampling frames, which can be omitted from the equation if they are equal or constant across time (note that each x_{ij}/t_{ij} term represents a mean). The variance of the logged RIRR is the sum of the inverse pre/post counts for each group and time period, which is calculated as follows:

$$v_{\ln(RIRR)} = \frac{1}{x_{11}} + \frac{1}{x_{10}} + \frac{1}{x_{01}} + \frac{1}{x_{00}} \tag{2}$$

This variance estimate is unadjusted for overdispersion, however, which is a common issue in count data. Thus, Wilson (2022) recommends the following overdispersion correction, based on the variance estimate in a quasi-Poisson model:

$$\Phi = \left(\frac{1}{\sum n_k - 4}\right)\sum \frac{s_k^2\,(n_k - 1)}{\overline{X}_k} \tag{3}$$

where $\overline{X}_k$ is the mean for each group/time period, S_k is the standard deviation for each group/time period, and n_k is the number of counts (contributing to the mean and standard deviation) for each group/time period. When the Φ value is greater than one, the variance estimate is multiplied by Φ to adjust for overdispersion. Otherwise, no overdispersion correction is needed.[3]

Though Equations (1)–(3) represent our main approach to effect size calculations, alternative methods were sometimes necessary.[4] Several studies

---

[3] Note that studies without pre-intervention observations generate incident rate ratios (IRR). These calculations follow the same approach but are simplified in that the IRR simply represents the rate of crime in post-intervention period for treatment group relative to the control group.

[4] The data needed to calculate the overdispersion correction proposed by Wilson (2022) were often unavailable. Following the approach used in recent meta-analyses in the field of criminology (Petersen & Lu, 2023; Petersen et al., 2023), we calculated the minimum, maximum, and average overdispersion correction for the studies that reported the necessary data to do so. We then used the average overdispersion correction from these studies to correct the standard errors for the remaining studies.

reported data in the form of regression coefficients estimated from ordinary least squares (OLS) regressions, binary logistic regressions, or negative binomial regressions. To convert OLS regression coefficients to RIRR values, we used the following equation (see Lum et al., 2020):

$$\ln(\text{RIRR}) = \ln\left(\frac{\bar{x}_c + B}{\bar{x}_C}\right) \tag{4}$$

where $\bar{x}_c$ is the post-intervention mean for the control group and B is the linear regression coefficient. The variance of the effect size is calculated using the following equation, where $\ln(RIRR)$ represents the natural log of the RIRR, SE_B represents the standard error of the linear regression coefficient, and B represents the regression coefficient itself:

$$v_{\ln(RIRR)} = \left(\frac{\ln(RIRR) * SE_B}{B}\right)^2 \tag{5}$$

At times, researchers also reported results in the form of logistic regression coefficients – for example – representing differences in the odds of criminal behavior for treatment individuals relative to control individuals (Flewelling et al., 2013). Though these outcomes are dichotomous, they can be expressed as risk ratios, corresponding to the ratio of the probability of the outcome for treatment individuals relative to control individuals. Given that risk ratios can also be considered censored counts (i.e., censored at 1), they can be meaningfully synthesized with RIRR estimates (Wilson, 2022; see also Lipsey & Wilson, 2000). Thus, to convert logistic regression coefficients to risk ratios, we used the following equation (see Lum et al., 2020):

$$ln(RR) = ln\left(\frac{OR}{(1-p) + (OR * p)}\right) \tag{6}$$

where OR is the odds ratio reported by the study authors and p is the probability of success (either in the treatment or in the control group depending on which group was placed in the numerator of the OR). The variance of the risk ratio is then calculated using the following equation, where $ln(RR)$ is the risk ratio calculated in Equation (6), $SE_{ln(OR)}$ is the standard error of the odds ratio reported by the study authors, and $ln(OR)$ is the natural log of the odds ratio reported by the study authors (Lum et al., 2020):

$$v_{\ln(RR)} = \left(\frac{ln(RR) * SE_{ln(OR)}}{ln(OR)}\right)^2 \tag{7}$$

Some studies also included count-based regression models (e.g., negative binomial regressions, for which see Mazerolle et al., 2019). Regression coefficients from these models naturally represent logged IRRs. Thus, these coefficients and their standard errors were taken directly from the regression tables presented by the study authors (see Wilson, 2022).[5]

Finally, we followed the same computational approaches as those described already to calculate effect sizes for spatial displacement and diffusion (see Weisburd et al., 2006). The only exception to this approach was for studies in which a buffer or catchment area was drawn around the treatment group but not the control group. In these situations, we followed the approach used by Telep and colleagues (2014) by comparing the treatment catchment areas directly to the control areas themselves.[6]

2.5 Data Synthesis

After calculating standardized effect sizes, researchers must make decisions regarding the type of meta-analytic model that is most appropriate for data synthesis. One such decision is the choice between use of a fixed effect or a random effects model (see Borenstein et al., 2010). Under a fixed effect model, the researcher assumes that there is a common or single population effect across all studies. In contrast, a random effects model allows for the possibility of variation in the true effect sizes across studies – in other words, the possibility that the true effect differs across subpopulations and treatment variations (see Borenstein et al., 2010; Lipsey & Wilson, 2000; Weisburd et al., 2022). Given differences in the characteristics of the TPP interventions included in our review, as well as the types of problems, places, and people targeted by these interventions, we assumed that the true effect of TPP would likely vary across studies. As such, we used random effects models with restricted maximum likelihood estimation to assess the impact of TPP on crime and disorder (see Langan et al., 2019; Lipsey & Wilson, 2000).[7] Additionally, we reported Q and I^2 statistics to quantify the degree of variation that exists between studies (see Higgins & Thompson, 2002).

---

[5] Note that several studies required variations of the methods described in this section or alternative methods altogether. Complete explanation and documentation of effect size calculations can be obtained directly from the authors of this Element.

[6] All effect size formulas were manually created in The R Project for Statistical Computing (R Core Team, 2023) based on equations presented in the technical Online Appendix of Lum and colleagues (2020) and Wilson (2022).

[7] It is also important to note that the random effects model will converge on the fixed effects model in the absence of between-study variability, and thus experts in the field typically recommend the use of a random effects model at baseline (see Borenstein et al., 2010; Weisburd et al., 2022).

A critical assumption of standard meta-analytic models is that of statistical independence between effect sizes (Borenstein et al., 2009; Lipsey & Wilson, 2000; Weisburd et al., 2022). However, the TPP evaluations included in our review frequently reported multiple outcome measures taken from the same set of places or people, leading to a violation of this assumption. A common approach to deal with this issue in meta-analysis is to employ a selection rule that prioritizes a single effect size from within each study (Matt, 1989; Tanner-Smith et al., 2016). For example, researchers may prioritize data sources that are considered more reliable, longer follow-up periods, or aggregate outcomes over individual crime types (see Matt, 1989; Petersen et al., 2022, 2023; Wilson et al., 2021).

In our main model specifications, we followed a similar approach by selecting the most general effect size reported in each study. In practice, this involved the selection of aggregate outcomes (e.g., total crime incidents or calls for service) over more specific measures of crime and disorder (e.g., drug crime, property crime, etc.). At times, however, this also involved the calculation of aggregate effect sizes by manually combining crime counts for specific types of offences that were reported individually (e.g., manually combining violent, property, and drug crime counts). Furthermore, we prioritized effect sizes pertaining to treatment variations in their most complete form. Several studies compared multiple treatment conditions to a shared control group (Eck & Wartell, 1998; Morton et al., 2018), for example where one treatment condition involved a letter sent to property owners encouraging them to implement changes at their properties and a second condition involved both the receipt of the letter and a face-to-face meeting with property owners. In these situations, we selected the effect corresponding to the full treatment implementation (i.e., letter and meeting). Our goal with these selection rules was to utilize as much information as possible from each study, in order to provide an overall estimate of the effect of TPP interventions when implemented in their fullest form. We followed the same process in selecting effect sizes corresponding to individual forms of crime and disorder as well. This allowed us to assess the differential impacts of TPP across more homogeneous subgroups of outcomes.[8]

Though the use of a selection rule is common, there is understandable concern that judgmental factors may result in the selection of effect sizes that are overly favorable or unfavorable to treatment (see Braga et al., 2019a; Matt, 1989). Thus, to ensure that our selection rule did not introduce bias into our

---

[8] Note also that when both incident and calls-for-service data were available, we prioritized incident data, given research to suggest that calls for service may become inflated when police build relationships with community members (see Weisburd et al., 2021; see also Lawrence et al., 2019).

findings, we replicated each standard meta-analytic model using robust variance estimation (RVE), which allows for the inclusion of all relevant effect sizes nested within each study. Increasingly used in meta-analyses in the natural and social sciences, RVE is an approach that is capable of handling correlated effect size structures. It does this by adjusting the weight of each effect size based on the number of effect sizes nested within a study and their average variance (Hedges et al., 2010; Tanner-Smith et al., 2016). Operationally, all effect sizes within a single study receive the same weight, with these weights becoming smaller as the number of nested effect sizes increases (see Hedges et al., 2010; Tanner-Smith et al., 2016). Ultimately, RVE helps to ensure that studies with more reported outcomes are not overrepresented in the analysis.[9]

2.6 Subgroup Analyses

Information about the contexts in which treatment is most and least effective is critical to the policy implications of meta-analysis (Johnson et al., 2015). Thus, an additional objective of this review was to explore factors that may moderate the effect of TPP interventions on crime and disorder. Specifically, we examined differences in effect size estimates across various forms of legal levers, the quantity and quality of partnerships (e.g., cooperative versus coercive, number of partners utilized), the targets of the interventions (e.g., micro-places, macro-places, people), and the research methodologies (experimental versus quasi-experimental). To conduct these analyses, we used the analog to the analysis of variance (ANOVA) method for categorical moderator variables (Hedges, 1982; Lipsey & Wilson, 2000) and meta-regression models for continuous or numeric moderator variables (Hedges & Olkin, 1985; Higgins et al., 2020).

2.7 Publication Bias

The potential for selective publication of research results – otherwise known as the "file-drawer" problem (Rosenthal, 1979, p. 638) – is a threat to the validity of any systematic review and meta-analysis (Rothstein, 2008). Though our search strategies covered a variety of gray literature databases,[10] it is always possible that research failing to produce significant results becomes discarded, ultimately biasing the completeness of the information included in a systematic review. To test for this potential, we used three approaches. First, we conducted a moderator analysis comparing average effect sizes for published and unpublished reports.

---

[9] Standard meta-analytic models and tests for publication bias were estimated using the "metafor" package (Viechtbauer, 2010) in The R Project for Statistical Computing (R Core Team, 2023). RVE models were estimated using the "robumeta" package (Fisher & Tipton, 2015).

[10] See the GPD search method at https://gpd.uq.edu.au/wp-content/uploads/2023/06/GPD-2023-Building-the-Evidence-Base.pdf.

Second, we generated funnel plots with trim-and-fill analyses to test for asymmetries in treatment effects based on the precision of the estimates (Duval & Tweedie, 2000). Third, we conducted an Egger's regression test to determine whether a linear relationship existed between the size of the observed effects and the size of their standard errors (Egger et al., 1997).

2.8 Summary Comments

In this section, we described the methods used to conduct our systematic review and meta-analysis of TPP interventions. Our review captures experimental and quasi-experimental evidence obtained through an exhaustive search and screening process and summarized using effect sizes that compare the pre- to post-intervention change in crime for treatment groups to the pre- to post-intervention change in crime for control groups. In Section 3, we present and discuss the main results of our systematic review and meta-analysis. Specifically, we discuss the characteristics of our included studies, the overall effect of TPP interventions on crime and disorder outcomes, and the robustness of our findings to different constraints and specifications.

3 Results

Measurement of program performance is a critical element of evidence-based crime policy (Lum & Koper, 2017; Sherman, 1998). As one of the most promising innovations in modern policing (Weisburd & Braga, 2019), TPP, along with a comprehensive understanding of its effects on crime and disorder, holds important implications for police practice. Meta-analytic results are uniquely suited for this purpose, given their ability to move discussion "away from individual studies toward an overview of the whole body of research on a given topic" (Lipsey & Wilson, 2000, p. 167). Accordingly, this section presents the main results of our systematic review and meta-analysis on TPP interventions. We first describe the characteristics of our included studies, followed by a discussion of our meta-analytic findings. Within this, we report estimates of the total effect of TPP interventions on crime and disorder as well as the effect of TPP interventions on specific forms of crime and disorder. We also examine the potential for bias in our results based on methodological quality and publication status. Ultimately, this section provides evidence of the general effectiveness of TPP as a crime prevention and reduction strategy.

3.1 Results of the Search

In total, our search and screening method generated twenty-four studies reported across thirty-nine documents. In the corpus of the twenty-four included studies, two studies contributed multiple independent comparisons (Hope, 1994; Warpenius & Holmila, 2008). Thus, for the purposes of this Element, we count a total of twenty-seven independent TPP partnership interventions for analysis (see Online Appendix). Summary study characteristics can be seen in Table 1. Seventy-five percent ($n = 18$) of eligible studies were conducted in the United States, with 44 percent ($n = 8$) of these studies taking place in California. The remaining studies were conducted in Australia (17 percent, $n = 4$), Finland (4 percent, $n = 1$), and the United Kingdom (4 percent, $n = 1$). Approximately 75 percent of eligible studies were also classified as published research evaluations (e.g., published journal articles, books, or book chapters), while 25 percent were classified as unpublished dissertations, theses, or reports.

From a methodological perspective, eligible studies were primarily characterized by quasi-experimentation or non-random assignment to treatment

Table 1 Summary study characteristics

Characteristic	N	%
Country		
United States	18	75.0
Australia	4	16.6
Finland	1	4.2
United Kingdom	1	4.2
Publication type		
Journal article	11	45.8
Book or book chapter	7	29.2
Dissertation or thesis	3	12.5
Report	3	12.5
Methodology		
Quasi-experiment (unmatched)	10	41.7
Quasi-experiment (matched)	7	29.1
Randomized experiment	6	25.0
Interrupted time series	1	4.2
Target of intervention		
Macro-places	12	50.0
Micro-places	11	45.8
People	1	4.2

Note: Categories are mutually exclusive.

(see Cook & Campbell, 1979). About 75 percent of studies were quasi-experiments of which 40 percent were considered "unmatched" quasi-experiments and 30 percent "matched" quasi-experiments. Here, "unmatched" indicates that control groups were not selected based on explicit considerations of comparability with treatment groups, while "matched" indicates that specific measures were taken to select comparable control groups (e.g., use of statistical matching procedures such as propensity score matching). For example, several "unmatched" studies selected control areas that appeared similar to treatment areas at face value, but without providing formal tests of baseline differences (Clarke & Bichler-Robertson, 1998; Felson et al., 1997; Sturgeon-Adams et al., 2005). Other "unmatched" designs compared crime changes in treatment areas to those of the rest of a jurisdiction or group at large (Elliott, 2007; Green, 1996; Koehle, 2011). Only six studies (25 percent) were classified as RCTs, which are considered the "gold standard" (Cartwright, 2007, p. 11; see also Sampson, 2010) for causal evaluation research. Thus, given the relative dearth of experimental evaluation in this area of research, along with prior evidence to suggest that methodological rigor often impacts study findings (Weisburd et al., 2001), we tested for significant differences in treatment effects across research methodologies in Section 3.5.

Finally, nearly all included studies implemented TPP interventions that targeted geographic areas. Fifty percent of studies evaluated TPP interventions targeting macrogeographic areas such as central business districts (Felson et al., 1997), neighborhoods (Koper et al., 2016), reporting districts (Tita et al., 2011), and towns (Warpenius & Holmila, 2008), while 46 percent of studies evaluated TPP interventions targeting microgeographic areas such as hotels/motels (Bichler et al., 2013), rental properties/dwelling units (Clarke & Bichler-Robertson, 1998; Eck & Wartell, 1998; Payne, 2017), and street blocks (Mazerolle et al., 2000). Only one study explicitly evaluated the effects of a TPP intervention on individuals, where Mazerolle and colleagues (Mazerolle et al., 2019) examined the effect of the Ability School Engagement Program (ASEP) on antisocial behavior among truant youth. We provide a summary of all eligible studies (both included and excluded from our meta-analysis) in the Online Appendix.

3.2 Studies Excluded from the Meta-analysis

Four eligible studies were not included in the meta-analysis. Three of these studies (Ferris et al., 2016; Putnam et al., 1993; White et al., 2003) reported insufficient information to calculate an effect size. Additionally, Morton, Luengen, and Mazerolle (2019) measured the effect of a TPP intervention on the reporting of suspicious/criminal behavior with the intent of the intervention being to *increase* reporting rates. Though the Morton et al. (2019) study met our eligibility criteria, we omitted it from our main analysis given that the intended effect was in the opposite direction from that of our remaining studies. Given the exclusion of these studies from the meta-analysis, we provide a brief overview of their key findings. These omitted studies are also summarized in the Online Appendix.

Ferris and colleagues (2016) evaluated the impact of Project STOP in Queensland on the amount of pseudoephedrine (PSE) products leaving pharmacies for methamphetamine production. Project STOP involved the mandatory recording of PSE sales into a database where all requests for the drug were entered, along with customer details/ID. Potentially suspicious transactions were flagged to the pharmacist prior to completing the sale, allowing the pharmacist to either proceed with the sale (referred to as a safety transaction) or deny the sale. Project STOP commenced in 2005 and within two months over a third of pharmacies in Queensland were using the registry. By 2008, 90 percent of all Queensland pharmacies were using Project STOP. Time series analyses revealed that once Project STOP reached 90 percent uptake, pharmacies in Queensland experienced a relatively stable rate of allowed PSE-based medication transactions. Similar trends were seen with the number of suspected pseudo-runners (i.e., individuals whose number of annual transactions breached the threshold), with declining rates of safety and denied transactions over time. However, the number of clandestine lab detections followed a different trend. While the number of detections initially decreased between 2004 and 2008, there was a significant upturn mid 2008 through to 2009. The number of clandestine detections declined after this time, but the decrease was nonsignificant.

White and colleagues (2003) examined the effectiveness of the Comprehensive Homicide Initiative on the prevalence of lethal violence in Richmond, California. The initiative involved a broad range of problem-oriented and community policing strategies. There was one TPP component whereby the Richmond Police, the City Attorney, and the Richmond Housing Authority collectively developed a model lease agreement to assist with code enforcement and nuisance abatement at residential addresses. Interrupted time series analyses comparing homicide trends in Richmond to seventy-five other cities in California showed that the decline in homicide was unique to Richmond.

Putnam and colleagues (1993) assessed the impact of the Rhode Island Community Alcohol Abuse/Injury Prevention Project on alcohol-related arrests. Like White and colleagues (2003), this intervention comprised several components, including some TPP elements (such as the adoption of a responsible service of alcohol [RSA] policy, training for bar staff on dram shop liability laws, and increased enforcement and knowledge of liquor laws by police). Here, Putnam and colleagues (1993) found that arrest rates *increased* by 9 percent in the intervention site compared to the comparison sites. Similarly, alcohol-related arrests and DWIs (arrests for driving while intoxicated) also increased (by 11 percent and 4 percent, respectively). The authors note that this increase is likely due to increased law enforcement activities in the intervention area.

Lastly, Morton and colleagues (2018) examined the impact of Operation Galley on the reporting of drug-related activities across hotels located in Brisbane, Australia. Operation Galley randomly allocated inner-city hotels to one of three conditions. The first experimental condition (referred to as *Letter Only*) was where detectives sent hotel management a letter outlining relevant legislation and information regarding the civil and criminal liabilities of the hotel and its staff regarding drug offending on the premises. The second experimental condition (*Operation Galley*) included the distribution of the letter as well as a meeting with the Combined Agency Response Team (CART) consisting of detectives and Queensland Fire and Emergency Services (QFES) officers. The CART team aimed to engage hotel managers and staff in a partnership approach by explaining the laws and their obligation to report suspicious drug activity. Hotels assigned to the control condition received a business-as-usual approach. The results showed significant differences between the three conditions both during and following the intervention. Specifically, hotels in the Operation Galley condition generated significantly more notifications to police than the letter only or control condition at both time points. Operation Galley hotels also saw a greater number of search warrants executed and drug crime reports. These findings suggest a greater willingness among hoteliers to act as intelligence sources when efforts are made to develop a partnership with police.

3.3 Results of the Meta-analysis

In total, there was sufficient information to calculate at least one standardized effect size for twenty-three of our twenty-seven independent tests of TPP. In twenty of these evaluations, we were able to calculate effect sizes representing the main effect of the intervention on crime and disorder, while in nine evaluations we were able to calculate an effect size representing the impact of the intervention on spatial displacement. One study, which included three independent comparisons (Hope, 1994), provided sufficient information to calculate effect sizes for spatial displacement only, and thus this study is included in our displacement analysis but omitted from our main analysis.

The results of our analysis for crime and disorder can be seen in the forest plot presented in Figure 1. Here, individual point estimates represent the effect size and 95 percent confidence interval for each study, with the size of the points denoting the weight that the study received in the overall analysis (i.e., larger points indicate greater weight). Effect sizes to the left of the reference or no effect line indicate decreases in crime and disorder for treatment groups relative to control groups and are considered favorable to treatment. The diamond at the bottom of the plot represents the overall mean effect size across studies, which is statistically significant if it does not overlap with the reference or no effect line. Finally, Q and I^2 statistics – which quantify heterogeneity and between-study variability – are displayed in the bottom-left corner of the plot.

Overall, the results of our meta-analysis indicate that TPP interventions are associated with a statistically significant 25 percent ($p < 0.01$) relative reduction in crime and disorder, with confidence intervals ranging from a 38 percent relative reduction to a 9 percent relative reduction (see Figure 1). Accordingly, TPP interventions display consistent and substantively meaningful impacts on crime and disorder. Of the twenty studies included in this analysis, seventeen provided results favorable to treatment conditions (i.e., indicating a decrease in crime for treatment groups relative to control groups) and six suggested statistically significant treatment effects.[11] Despite this consistency, however, there remains a statistically significant degree of between-study heterogeneity (Q = 148.98,

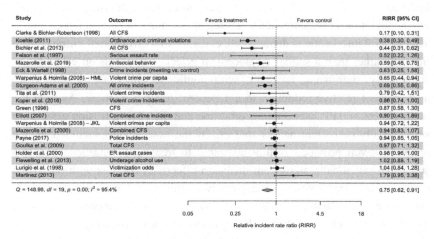

Figure 1 Forest plot of TPP effects on crime and disorder.

Note: CFS = Calls for service; ER = Emergency room.

---

[11] Note that this count is based on our effect size calculations, which may not always correlate with effects that the original study authors concluded to be statistically significant.

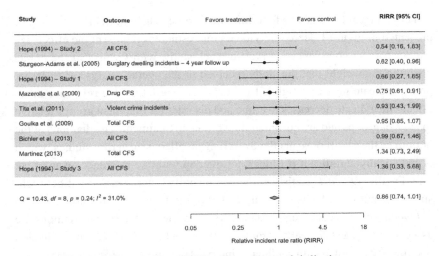

Figure 2 Forest plot of TPP effects on spatial displacement.
Note: CFS = Calls for service.

df = 19, p < 0.01), with over 95 percent of the total variability in results being attributable to between-study variability. This suggests that, though consistent in implication, important sources of variation may exist for TPP interventions.

Figure 2 displays the results of our spatial displacement analysis. The mean effect size for the nine studies included in this analysis indicates that TPP interventions are associated with a 14 percent decrease in crime and disorder for treatment buffer/catchment areas relative to control buffer/catchment areas. That is, TPP interventions demonstrate evidence of a diffusion of crime control benefits rather than a spatial displacement effect. This diffusion effect is not statistically significant, however, with confidence intervals ranging from a 26 percent relative reduction to a 1 percent relative increase. As with the main effects of TPP interventions on crime and disorder, diffusion effects are substantively consistent across studies. Of the nine studies included in this analysis, seven provided results favorable to treatment conditions and two suggested statistically significant diffusion effects. In contrast with our crime reduction results, however, heterogeneity in this model was not statistically significant (Q = 10.43, df = 8, p = 0.24), and only 31 percent of the total variability in results was attributable to between-study variability.

3.4 Results by Crime Type and Target of Intervention

Though our main findings suggest substantively consistent impacts of TPP interventions on crime and disorder, they also suggest that there are important sources of variation in these effects. One such source of variation may be the type of problem that the intervention is intending to address. Our overall analyses combine a highly heterogeneous set of outcomes that all exist under the umbrella of "crime and disorder." For example, these findings synthesize various forms of aggregate, violent, property, drug, and disorder offenses – and thus it remains possible that the effect of TPP is dependent on the type of crime and disorder used for evaluation (see Mazerolle & Ransley, 2005). Typically, researchers explore sources of variation in meta-analytic models using moderator analyses (e.g., comparing effect sizes for studies with differential characteristics, on which see Lipsey & Wilson, 2000). However, our primary results prioritized the selection of the most general or aggregate effect size from each study, even when more specific forms of crime or disorder were measured. This was done, in part, to increase the homogeneity of outcomes; however, it also limits our ability to test for significant differences in effect sizes across crime types within the same model. Thus, to examine variation in these effects, we estimated separate meta-analytic models for aggregate, violent, property, and drug/disorder offenses, selecting the most general effect size for each crime type from all applicable studies (see Section 2).

Twelve of twenty studies included in our meta-analysis provided an aggregate measure of crime or disorder (see Figure 3). The most common form of measurement for these outcomes was combined calls for service (Bichler et al., 2013; Clarke & Bichler-Robertson, 1998; Goulka et al., 2009; Green, 1996; Martinez, 2013; Mazerolle et al., 2000), followed by police incidents or violations (Eck & Wartell, 1998; Elliott, 2007; Koehle, 2011; Payne, 2017; Sturgeon-Adams et al., 2005), and self-reported victimization (Lurigio et al., 1998). The mean effect size for these studies corresponds to a statistically significant 29 percent ($p = 0.04$) relative

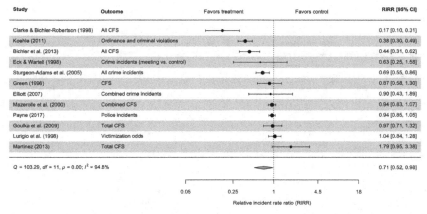

Figure 3 Forest plot of TPP effects on aggregate crime and disorder.
Note: CFS = Calls for service.

reduction in aggregate crime and disorder, with confidence intervals ranging from a 48 percent relative reduction to a 2 percent relative reduction. Ten of these twelve studies reported results favoring treatment (i.e., suggesting relative decreases in crime for treatment groups), and four of these effect sizes were statistically significant. However, even when limiting the analysis to aggregate measures of crime and disorder, there remains a significant amount of between-study heterogeneity ($Q = 103.29$, $df = 11$, $p < 0.01$), with 95 percent of the total variability in results stemming from between-study variability.

Eleven of twenty studies provided a measure of violent crime (see Figure 4). The most common form of measurement for these outcomes was combined violent crime incidents (Elliott, 2007; Koper et al., 2016; Tita et al., 2011; Warpenius & Holmila, 2008), followed by combined violent calls for service (Goulka et al., 2009; Martinez, 2013; Mazerolle et al., 2000), serious assaults (Felson et al., 1997), street robberies (Lurigio et al., 1998), and emergency room assault cases (Holder et al., 2000). Across these studies, the mean effect size corresponds to a 5 percent ($p = 0.16$) reduction in violent crime for treatment groups relative to control groups. However, this effect is not statistically significant, with confidence intervals ranging from an 11 percent relative reduction to a 2 percent relative increase. Seven of these eleven studies reported results favoring treatment, though only one effect size was statistically significant. Additionally, there was a nonsignificant degree of between-study variability in this model ($Q = 15.02$, $df = 10$, $p = 0.13$), with only 14 percent of the total variance stemming from between-study variability.

Only six studies measured the effect of TPP interventions on property crime (see Figure 5). The most common form of measurement for property crime was combined property-related calls for service (Goulka et al., 2009; Martinez, 2013;

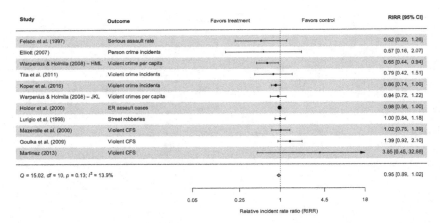

Figure 4 Forest plot of TPP effects on violent crime.

Note: CFS = Calls for service; ER = Emergency room.

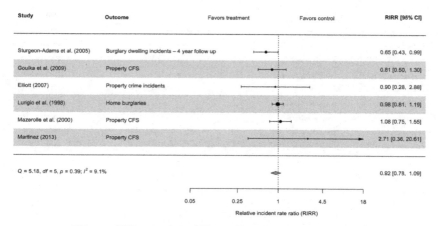

Figure 5 Forest plot of TPP effects on property crime.
Note: CFS = Calls for service.

Mazerolle et al., 2000), followed by burglary incidents (Lurigio et al., 1998; Sturgeon-Adams et al., 2005) and combined property crime incidents (Elliott, 2007). The mean effect size for these studies corresponds to a nonsignificant 8 percent ($p = 0.35$) reduction in property crime for treatment groups relative to control groups, with confidence intervals ranging from a 22 percent relative reduction to a 9 percent relative increase. Four of these six studies reported results favorable to treatment; however, only one effect size was statistically significant. As with violent crime, there was a nonsignificant degree of between-study variability in this model ($Q = 5.18$, $df = 5$, $p = 0.39$), with just 9 percent of the total variation stemming from between-study variability.

Finally, eight of twenty studies measured some form of drug or disorder offense (see Figure 6). Most commonly, this involved drug/disorder calls for service (Goulka et al., 2009; Martinez, 2013; Mazerolle et al., 2000), followed by drug or alcohol use (Flewelling et al., 2013; Lurigio et al., 1998), DWI (Holder et al., 2000), antisocial behavior (Mazerolle et al., 2019), and combined disorder incidents (Elliott, 2007). Across these eight studies, the mean effect size corresponds to a nonsignificant 15 percent ($p = 0.16$) relative reduction in drug/disorder offenses, with confidence intervals ranging from a 33 percent relative reduction to a 7 percent relative increase. In total, five of eight studies reported results favorable to treatment groups, with two statistically significant effect sizes. Results for drug/disorder offenses displayed a significant amount of between-study variability ($Q = 22.53$, $df = 7$, $p < 0.01$), with approximately 71 percent of the total variability in results being attributable to between-study variability.

Criminology

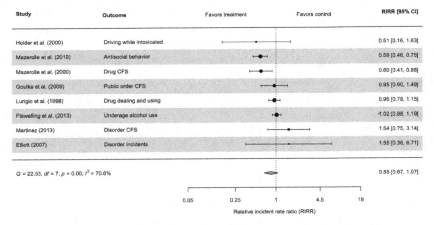

Figure 6 Forest plot of TPP effects on drug crime and disorder.
Note: CFS = Calls for service.

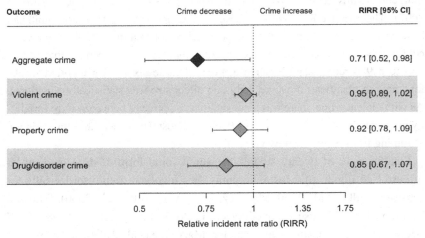

Figure 7 Summary of TPP effects across crime types.

Taking the results of Figures 3–6 together, our results point to variation in the impact of TPP interventions across different forms of crime and disorder (see Figure 7). Specifically, our results suggest that TPP interventions may produce the strongest deterrent effect on drug/disorder offenses and the weakest deterrent effect on violent offenses. Even so, our estimates suggest deterrent effects of TPP on each form of crime and disorder analyzed. Thus, we observe the strongest and most robust preventive effects of TPP interventions when combining these measures into aggregate analyses of crime and disorder. Accordingly, only the effect of TPP interventions on aggregate crime and disorder was statistically significant when estimated individually, though this result should not be surprising. Aggregate analyses benefit from the largest number of studies and the most precise effect estimates, and, therefore, greater statistical power than analyses of individual crime types. Indeed, post hoc power analyses suggested that – given our observed effect sizes, average sample sizes, number of studies, and degree of between-study variability – our probability of detecting a significant effect for individual crime types was as low as 6–19 percent across outcomes.[12] As such, the statistical significance of these individual crime type models should be interpreted with caution.

One final element of TPP interventions that may be fundamental to their impact on crime and disorder is the target of the intervention. The majority of included interventions targeted geographic places rather than people, though there was variation in the size of the geographic areas targeted. To examine differences in treatment effect based on the target of the intervention, we used a categorical moderator analysis to compare average effect sizes between macrogeographic areas, microgeographic areas, and people. The results of this analysis can be seen in Figure 8, where each bar represents the mean effect size associated with each target, the dotted line represents the reference or no effect line, and the confidence intervals for each bar represent the range of likely values for the associated effect size. Effect sizes with confidence intervals that overlap the reference line are not statistically significant, while effect sizes with confidence intervals that overlap one another do not significantly differ. Finally, effect sizes below the reference line indicate relative decreases in crime (i.e., effects favorable to treatment), while effects above the reference line indicate relative increases in crime (i.e., effects favorable to control).

Consistent with the literature on hot-spots policing and crime and place (see Sherman & Weisburd, 1995; Weisburd, 2015; Weisburd & Eck, 2004; Weisburd & Majmundar, 2018), interventions targeting microgeographic areas were associated with larger crime reductions than interventions targeting macrogeographic areas (see Figure 8). Specifically, microgeographic studies were associated with a 29 percent relative crime reduction (95 percent CI: −48 percent, −2 percent), while macrogeographic studies were associated with a 20 percent

---

[12] In other words, assuming that our observed effect sizes and levels of heterogeneity are correct, these are the power levels of our random effects models. To examine this, we used the metapower package in The R Project for Statistical Computing (Griffin, 2021). Given that this package does not handle RIRR effect sizes, we treated the RIRR as an odds ratio and converted it to a Cohen's *d* estimate using the Cox method (see Sanchez-Meca et al., 2003). While we acknowledge that this is not a precise estimate of statistical power, it does reflect the underpowered nature of our individual crime type models.

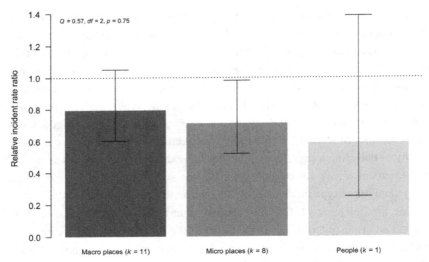

Figure 8 Moderator analysis by target of TPP intervention.

Note: k = Number of studies, Q = The X^2 statistic of the moderator analysis.

relative crime reduction (95 percent CI: −40 percent, 5 percent). Though there was only one person-based study, it was associated with the largest effect size, a 41 percent relative crime reduction (95 percent CI: −75 percent, 39 percent). Despite this, the target of the intervention was not a significant moderator of treatment effects (Q = 0.57, df = 2, p = 0.75).

3.5 Risk of Bias

Variation in methodological quality and selective publication of study findings create the potential for bias in any systematic review and meta-analysis (Rothstein, 2008; Shadish & Heinsman, 1997; Weisburd et al., 2001). As noted, the majority of our included studies were both quasi-experimental in nature and published in peer-reviewed journals, books, or book chapters. To examine the impact of these characteristics on our overall findings, we conducted categorical moderator analyses comparing mean effect sizes between research methodologies and publication status. Additionally, we generated funnel plots and conducted Egger's regression tests to further examine the potential for publication bias.

The results of our moderator analysis for research methodology – comparing average effect sizes for unmatched quasi-experiments, matched quasi-experiments, and randomized experiments – can be seen in Figure 9. Unmatched quasi-experiments were associated with the largest crime reductions (−35 percent) followed by randomized experiments (−20 percent) and matched

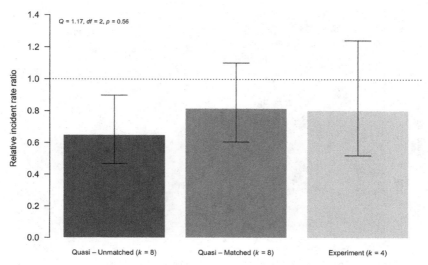

Figure 9 Moderator analysis by research methodology.

Note: k = Number of studies, Q = The X^2 statistic of the moderator analysis.

quasi-experiments (−18 percent), but the difference between these groups was not statistically significant (Q = 1.17, df = 2, p = 0.56). Despite this, unmatched quasi-experiments were the only subgroup to demonstrate statistically significant individual effects (95 percent CI: −53 percent, −10 percent), while randomized experiments (95 percent CI: −48 percent, 24 percent) and matched quasi-experiments (95 percent CI: −39 percent, 10 percent) did not. In other words, methodologically "weaker" studies appeared to produce more favorable results; however, these differences may have been due to chance.

To test for publication bias, a funnel plot displaying the primary effect sizes from each study can be seen in Figure 10. Under the presence of publication bias, we would expect to see asymmetry in the plot, such that an excess of studies would appear on the left side of the plot as the standard error increases (see Anzures-Cabrera & Higgins, 2010). While a small degree of asymmetry can be seen in Figure 10, our trim-and-fill analysis suggested that this asymmetry was not statistically significant, and no additional effect sizes were imputed into the plot (similarly, an Egger's regression test also failed to detect significant asymmetry, b = −0.13, p = 0.26). Our moderator analysis comparing average effect sizes for published and unpublished studies also pointed to a lack of publication bias. Published studies were associated with a 26 percent relative reduction in crime (with confidence intervals ranging from a 42 percent relative reduction to a 7 percent relative reduction), while unpublished studies were associated with a 22 percent relative reduction in crime (with confidence intervals ranging from

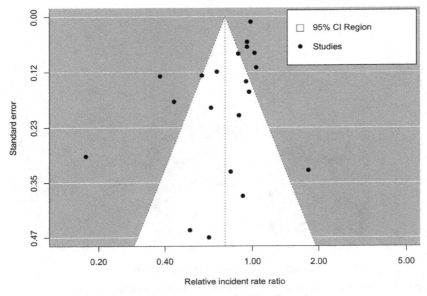

Figure 10 Funnel plot of TPP effect sizes.

Note: CI = Confidence interval.

a 46 percent relative reduction to a 14 percent relative increase), a difference that was small and not statistically significant ($Q = 0.07$, $df = 1$, $p = 0.79$). Thus, across all analyses, any potential bias in our results related to methodology or publication status appears to be small.

3.6 Sensitivity Analyses

For the purpose of statistical independence, all of our results up to this point have included only one effect size from each study. However, we were often able to calculate multiple nested effect sizes corresponding to various forms of crime and disorder, treatment variations, and follow-up lengths. In total, we calculated seventy-six effect sizes, fifty-seven (75 percent) of which corresponded to crime and disorder outcomes and nineteen (25 percent) of which corresponded to tests of spatial displacement. Across the twenty studies examining the impact of TPP interventions on crime and disorder, there was an average of 2.85 effect sizes per study. Across the nine studies examining the impact of TPP interventions on spatial displacement, there was an average of 2.11 effect sizes per study. To test the sensitivity of our primary results to the selection of a single effect size per study, and to incorporate all calculated effect sizes into a single analysis, we also replicated our analyses using RVE models.

Table 2 Robust variance estimation sensitivity analyses

	% crime reduction	95% CI	k	n	I^2
Crime/disorder	-24.30^{**}	$-36.47, -9.8$	20	57	78.52
Spatial displacement	-15.62	$-38.97, 16.66$	9	19	0.00

Note: k = number of studies, n = number of effect sizes, I^2 = percent of heterogeneity attributable to between-study variance.
$^{**}p < 0.01$.

The results of our RVE models largely support those of our primary analyses and can be seen in Table 2. For the crime and disorder model, results indicate that TPP interventions are associated with a statistically significant 24 percent ($p < 0.01$) relative crime reduction (down from a 25 percent relative reduction in our primary model), with confidence intervals ranging from a 36 percent relative reduction to a 10 percent relative reduction. For the spatial displacement model, results indicate that TPP interventions are associated with approximately a 16 percent relative crime reduction (i.e., decrease in crime and disorder for treatment buffer/catchment areas relative to control buffer/catchment areas), up from a 14 percent relative reduction in our primary model. Once again, however, these displacement results are not statistically significant, with confidence intervals ranging from a 39 percent relative reduction to a 17 percent relative increase. Heterogeneity remains high for the crime and disorder model, with 79 percent of the total variability being attributable to between-study variation, though there is a lack of between-study heterogeneity in the spatial displacement model.

Our analyses by crime type, target of the intervention, and examination of potential biases were also robust to the use of RVE. Similar to our primary results, the effects of TPP interventions were largest for general measures of crime (-22 percent) and drug/disorder offenses (-13 percent). Moreover, neither the target of the intervention nor the research methodology nor the publication status was a significant moderator of treatment effect in our RVE models. Finally, we conducted several additional sensitivity analyses to test the robustness of these findings to various specifications. First, we omitted studies that required the use of effect size calculations which differed from those described in Section 3. For example, several studies reported results using line graphs or plots without precise point estimates (Hope, 1994; Warpenius & Holmila, 2008), while others reported rates of crime/disorder per 100,000 people (Felson et al., 1997). For these studies, we were forced to take measures such as digitizing line graphs and converting reported rates into counts using population estimates (e.g., in order to calculate the appropriate effect size variance).[13] Given that these conversions may carry some degree of error, we reestimated our models after omitting these studies. Results of these analyses remained substantively consistent with our overall findings, with statistically significant relative crime reductions ranging from 30 percent to 32 percent and nonsignificant diffusion effects ranging from 10 percent to 12 percent, depending on model specification.

3.7 Summary Comments

In this section, we presented the main results of our systematic review and meta-analysis on the preventive effects of TPP interventions. Our findings indicate that TPP leads to significant and meaningful reductions in crime and disorder without displacing it to nearby areas. Additionally, TPP appears to produce the strongest and most robust effects on general measures of crime and drug/disorder offenses, as well as when targeted at people and microgeographic places. Further, our results provide some promising evidence to suggest that TPP can also reduce both violent and property crime and may remain effective when targeted at macrogeographic areas. Our findings are also robust to a number of potential biasing factors, such as methodological rigor and selective publication. Accordingly, these results provide strong evidence in support of the efficacy of TPP as both a general and a targeted crime prevention strategy. In the following sections, we examine the characteristics of TPP interventions in more depth, assessing the degree to which key characteristics of these interventions affect program effectiveness.

4 The Role of Legal Levers

One of the necessary mechanisms of TPP interventions is the activation, escalation, or redirection of a third party's legal levers. Legal levers are broadly defined as the legal powers possessed by third parties that create a crime control or crime prevention capacity that is otherwise unavailable to police. In contrast to criminal law, which creates offenses enforced via the criminal justice system (police, prosecutors, criminal courts), regulatory law creates frameworks for the orderly conduct of legal activities and is enforced by regulatory authorities. Private law, which has a different focus from criminal and regulatory laws, involves disputes between individuals such as those about contracts or negligence and is enforced by the affected individual (Cheh, 1998; Mazerolle & Ransley, 2005; Ransley, 2016). In contrast to many other policing approaches (see Section 1), legal levers

---

[13] To digitize line graphs, we used Engage Digitizer (http://markummitchell.github.io/engauge-digitizer/), which has been used in recent systematic reviews and meta-analyses (Petersen et al., 2023; Tantry et al., 2021).

in TPP are drawn from those regulatory and private legal frameworks to supplement or bolster the criminal justice powers already held by police.

By drawing on the non–criminal (i.e., civil) justice powers of third-party partners, police can extend the range of tactics available to address problem people or places that lead to crime and disorder by accessing, influencing, activating, escalating, or redirecting these legal levers. As described by Mazerolle and colleagues (2016, p. 9),

> examples of legal levers include conduct licensing (e.g., firearm ownership), business licensing (e.g., liquor, pharmacy or weapon sales), mandatory reporting (e.g., chemical sales, child abuse), orders to control behavior (e.g., gang or domestic violence injunctions, truancy regulations), orders under standard property codes (e.g., building, fire, health and safety, noise codes), and specific property controls (e.g., drug nuisance abatement, brothel regulations).

Legal levers define and shape TPP interventions in two ways; first, they indicate which third parties might be helpful partners given their powers that may be leveraged; second, the legal lever provisions set out the specific procedural aspects of a TPP intervention, including the required legal processes, the possible legal outcomes, and the consequences of lever usage. In each case, the legal lever is held by a non-police third party who has legal authority to implement or enforce the lever. For example, liquor licensing authorities can enforce compliance with licensing conditions affecting bar owners (e.g., staff training, hours of service, age restrictions, refusal of supply to intoxicated patrons, license to operate), ultimately aimed at regulating behaviors of patrons of licensed establishments. Formal regulations constitute this legal lever. Bar owners also have legal levers, in the form of the right to refuse service or to eject unruly patrons, with these levers sourced from contract or tort law, as well as from liquor regulation. Collectively, these levers can extend the reach of criminal justice powers held by police (e.g., arrest for assault or disorder). Importantly, while police powers tend to be retrospective in that they are usually activated only after an incident has occurred, regulatory and private law measures can be preventive, aimed at reducing opportunities for crimes to be committed. In TPP, therefore, police can address the conditions that allow a crime problem to flourish by partnering with a third party holding a lever affecting individuals, groups of individuals, or characteristics of places or geographic areas (see also Mazerolle et al., 2016).

As discussed in Section 1, the availability of legal levers has been enhanced by the expansion of the state's regulatory activity over the past century (Braithwaite, 2000; Mazerolle & Ransley, 2005), involving new or extended domains of regulation (e.g., tobacco sales and marketing, environmental protection, harassment and vilification, e-safety) and the creation of new regulators to oversee them. Such regulators typically have a range of civil powers, including licensing and reporting requirements, and conduct orders (e.g., rectification, non-association, or forfeiture orders). This growth and innovation in regulation provides much of the variety of TPP levers now accessed by police.

Legal levers can be categorized by (a) their source of legal authority, (b) the extent of their application, and (c) the type of legal outcomes or consequences they may produce. Sources of legal authority include statutes, regulation/subordinate legislation, contract or tort law, while the extent of application can be either general or targeted (e.g., specific population, area, parties to contract, those with duty of care). Depending on the legal framework and the third party, the types of legal consequence can be criminal, civil, or administrative in nature, including fines, license revocation, incarceration, eviction, property forfeiture, orders for compensation or damages, infringement notices, injunctions, and refusal of entry into or ejection from licensed premises. We identified several different types of regulatory law, ordinance, and civil code used in the TPP partnerships included in this review. For illustrative purposes, we draw on the legal provisions of all twenty-seven eligible interventions, although the moderator analyses in Section 4.4 draw on just twenty of those studies (see discussion in Section 3.1).

In our review, we identified interventions that involved laws pertaining to permits to operate (Bichler et al., 2013; Koehle, 2011), public safety codes such as fire and health (Bichler et al., 2013; Clarke & Bichler-Robertson, 1998; Elliott, 2007; Goldkamp & Vîlcică, 2008; Green, 1996; Martinez, 2013; Mazerolle et al., 2000; Morton et al., 2019), building and property codes (Corsaro et al., 2013; Eck & Wartell, 1998; Hope, 1994; Goldkamp & Vîlcică, 2008; Green, 1996; Koper et al., 2016; Lurigio et al., 1998; Martinez, 2013; Mazerolle et al., 2000; Payne, 2017; White et al., 2003), school attendance (Bennett et al., 2018), parole/probation violations (Koper et al., 2016; Tita et al., 2011), evictions for tenancy violations (White et al., 2003), liquor licensing accords/agreements that specified operating conditions of bars, clubs, pubs, and dram shops (Felson et al., 1997; Flewelling et al., 2013; Holder et al., 2000; Putnam et al., 1993; Warpenius et al., 2010), mandatory reporting of sales of precursors for drugs (Ferris et al., 2016; Mazerolle et al., 2017), non-association injunctions (Goulka et al., 2009), and access orders such as those relating to alley gates (Sturgeon-Adams et al., 2005). In this section, we examine these legal levers in three categories, depending on the nature of law used. The categories are enforcement of a type of code or ordinance, liquor license enforcement, and civil (noncriminal) orders to control behaviors.

4.1 Code/Ordinance Enforcement

By code or ordinance enforcement we mean that the TPP intervention involved police partnering with a regulatory authority holding powers under noncriminal legal codes having a broad community effect. For example, one study involved police partnering with city authorities to reduce call-outs to budget motels recording excessive levels of drug offending, noise complaints, non-payment, and other disturbances. City code enforcement officers inspected problematic premises identified in police data, and where motel operators were uncooperative, six city agencies (attorney, fire, finance, police, planning and building, and community development) developed a permit to operate process, where permits could be suspended for failing to comply with various code requirements (Bichler et al., 2013). Another example (Hope, 1994) targeted drug dealing locations and associated disorder by increasing standard policing efforts coupled with identifying owners of residential rental properties where such activity was happening. Owners of problem properties were contacted by police and proactively visited by a city enforcement official who worked with them to rectify the property, evict problem tenants, or condemn the property as unsafe (drawing on civil property or housing codes). In one case, the company providing finance to the property owner was persuaded to threaten foreclosure in an example of a private contractual level being harnessed. Other code enforcement levers involved multiagency teams comprising housing, fire, public works, power, and rodent control officers (Mazerolle et al., 2000), fire and emergency services agencies (Morton et al., 2018), and housing, parole and probation and prosecutor's officers (Tita et al., 2011). Two studies involved pharmacy boards, responsible for regulating individual pharmacies and their owners, in an attempt to reduce diversion of methamphetamine precursors (Ferris et al., 2016; see also Hattingh et al., 2016).

While the targeted problems and partners differed, these studies had in common the involvement of other government agencies (whether city or state), charged with regulating some lawful activity (e.g., property ownership and rental, motel or hotel operation, or pharmacy operation). Regulations relevant to that activity were leveraged as a means to better control criminal offending. Typically, the legal levers involved the restriction or withdrawal of a right to operate (rentals, motels, pharmacies) or mandatory repair orders (rentals) which could be used as an explicit or implied threat or sanction for non-cooperation with police.

The precise activation process for this type of legal lever depends on the stipulations of the relevant law. Typically, non-compliance comes to the attention of the regulator through their own activities, complaints, or police reports. This will usually be followed by regulator action such as the issue of a notice requiring compliance or rectification which will often set out the consequences of non-compliance. A timeframe for compliance will be stipulated. Continued non-compliance triggers further action such as a financial penalty, withdrawal of a license or permit, or possibly forfeiture or property demolition. Some codes allow for the cutting off from services such as water or electricity, or the revocation of a permit to operate required (e.g., motel owners). As with most regulatory authority, there is considerable discretion in how the regulator approaches their role and the extent to which it involves persuasion and cooperation versus coercion and punishment (Ayres & Braithwaite, 1992). Court or tribunal proceedings may be required for some actions. Importantly, the enforcement power stays with the third-party.

There is considerable variation across the studies included in our review with regard to threshold requirements, time limits, and potential legal consequences. But what is important is that most of the code enforcement cases are triggered by the same type of initial notice to comply. However, in the pharmacy-based studies there are two levers, first professional registration and conduct regulation governing pharmacists' right to practice, and second, health legislation regarding the sale of legal drugs. The process for the first lever is like other regulatory codes, in that pharmacists are notified and required to respond to alleged instances of professional misconduct, before the lever of license restriction can be activated by a regulatory board or tribunal. The health regulations are activated by state health agencies and suspected infringements are investigated before fines and other penalties are issued, based on a civil standard of proof. In some instances, criminal law may also be contravened, and in these situations, the infringement is dealt with by standard criminal justice processes.

The police role in these code enforcement studies varied. Some interventions were driven by police, particularly those where the primary crime control targets were reductions in calls for service or reducing drug problems. For example, Clark and Bichler-Robertson (1998) describe how police analyzed arrest and service data for problem properties before partnering with city authorities to access their powers over code violations. They note that ultimately building and safety authorities assumed the lead role, but the police began and designed the initiative to deal with a crime problem. Other studies also involved police analyzing a crime problem and then forming joint responses with regulators (e.g., Elliott, 2007; Green, 1996; Martinez, 2013; Mazerolle et al., 2000; Payne, 2017; White et al., 2003). These initiatives were variously described as intelligence-led policing (Morton et al., 2018), team policing (Martinez, 2013), community policing (Hope, 1994) or POP (Clarke & Bichler-Robertson, 1998), indicating that they were seen as police-led initiatives. In some studies, the joint initiative seemed to be less police-driven; for example, Koehle (2011) describes an initiative as being formed by the relevant Borough authority, with representation from police along with ordinance and health enforcers. In others, the driving force appeared to be external. For example, Tita and colleagues (2011) describe a research project in the US, initiated with National Institute of Justice funding, to replicate a successful gun-violence reduction project established in Boston. The project was driven by crime analysts employed by a project working group, with police engaged as partners. Similarly, in other included studies involving pharmacy regulation, the driver is also external, in the form of legislation requiring pharmacists to record sales and refuse sales of commonly used drug precursor products (Hattingh et al., 2016; Mazerolle et al., 2017). In these cases, the legislation clearly drove the establishment of the partnership. In Section 6 we examine whether these differences in police roles within TPP partnerships have any effect on the extent of coerciveness affecting partners.

4.2 Liquor Licensing Enforcement

Our second category of legal lever is liquor license enforcement. Here, the TPP intervention involves police partnering with licensing authorities to specifically target alcohol-related crime. For example, in one study police partnered with the liquor licensing authority and local bar operators to reduce assaults and other crimes in a night-time entertainment precinct (Felson et al., 1997). An Accord stipulating responsible service practices was developed cooperatively, but compliance was incentivized by the authority holding legal powers to investigate and close businesses. In Holder and colleagues (2000), the intervention involved increased police enforcement of drink-driving limits, increased enforcement of under-age and responsible service drinking limits, and the use of city zoning laws to control outlet density. This type of approach often targets young drinkers (e.g., Flewelling et al., 2013; Holmila & Warpenius, 2013), and also aims for community or group mobilization to support the intervention (Putnam et al., 1993).

The activation process for this group of studies is again dictated by the local liquor regulation. Typically, these TPP interventions involve joint teams or task-forces including licensing authorities, police and often others such as fire, safety, or health agencies. These teams conduct planned operations to detect non-compliance. In most cases this follows a similar pattern of inspection, and the issue of non-compliance notices. Depending on the jurisdiction action may be taken by several team members based on the type of non-compliance: e.g., liquor authority for breach of license conditions, fire or safety officers for over-crowding, police for other offending. The type of penalty will depend on who takes action, but the ultimate penalty for liquor authorities is withdrawal of the license to operate. There may be a right to challenge actions via an appeal process. Continued failure to comply may lead to suspension or cancellation of the licence by a board or tribunal, but also potentially to fines and criminal prosecution in some jurisdictions.

The presence of liquor regulation is central to these interventions, with the legal lever being license conditions relating to responsible service, hours of service, and under-age drinkers. The police role in these interventions varies. Several interventions were led by other agencies such as health or community organizations, with police enlisted as a partner (e.g., Flewelling et al., 2013; Holder et al., 2000; Putnam et al., 1993; Warpenius et al., 2010) indeed, of our included studies in this category only one was clearly police-initiated and led (Felson et al., 1997). One effect of this is that for this type of intervention, harm reduction and community development are often the goals, rather than crime control. Instead, law enforcement is a tactic to achieve health or community outcomes. While all included studies in this category involved law enforcement, the police role was largely secondary, with the regulatory enforcement a tool primarily intended to achieve other purposes.

4.3 Civil Actions/Orders

The third category of legal lever we have labelled civil action, by which we mean the use of a legal power to make orders about the conduct of a particular person or place. This category can be distinguished from code or ordinance enforcement because here a civil law authorizes the creation of a positive duty relating to the individual, rather than codes which tend to apply generally to the community or large sections of it (e.g., property owners). For example, Eck and Wartell (1998) describe an intervention targeting drug dealing by housing tenants. The legal lever drawn on was the ability of the city to take civil action against the landlord for a nuisance abatement order, which obliges the landlord to control the conduct and activities of the tenant so as to end the nuisance, often by tenant eviction. Police partnered with city authorities to identify landlords of problem premises and assist them to reduce the nuisance and avoid the civil action. Nuisance abatement orders were also used in another study, where the intervention was led by the state attorney's office and involved responses to drug houses (Lurigio et al., 1998). Similarly, in Koper and colleagues (2016), nuisance abatement orders targeting problem landlords were part of a comprehensive intervention designed to address gun violence that also include improved probation monitoring of offenders and community-based initiatives. In Goulka and colleagues (2009), police partnered with city attorneys to target gang-related crime, using a civil gang injunction which typically restricts an individual's association or movement with other gang members. Another study involved police partnering with schools to address chronic truanting/school absence by young people (Mazerolle et al., 2019). Education regulations allowed school principals to issue orders to parents requiring them to enforce school attendance. This order is issued administratively, but continued non-compliance is grounds for the imposition of a fine. Police were able to use the possibility of such a sanction to try to secure compliance from children and their parents.

These types of order can also target places. For example, one study involved a local authority access a prohibition order that enabled alley-gating in crime prone laneways which allowed for the installation of gates to physically block laneway access to make offending more difficult (Sturgeon-Adams et al., 2005). In this intervention, the order related to a specified location jointly identified by police and crime prevention officers. In this civil actions/orders category of legal levers, the lever is the order that can be made against individuals or locations. This order creates a positive duty for the recipient to comply, with non-compliance usually attracting fines or other penalties such as forfeiture. These levers often require the involvement of legal authorities, with a court required to issue the order (e.g., for nuisance abatement or gang injunctions). The truancy example (Mazerolle et al., 2019) differs in that the truancy order is administratively issued by a school principal, however non-compliance can lead to criminal enforcement. While legal authorities are often involved in the application of civil orders to control behaviors, the police role is typically important. This is not only because the problems targeted tend to be crimino-genic – such as those situations that promote drug or gang crime – but also because the problems targeted tend to be precursors to crime (such as school non-attendance, which is a known antecedent to youth criminality).

The activation process for these orders is typically the capacity of the third-party to apply to a court or tribunal for an order affecting an individual, group, or place under specific legislation (e.g., nuisance abatement or gang injunction laws). Such applications will require supporting evidence, the nature of which depends on the specific legislation. This means there needs to have been some kind of investigation, prior conduct, or intelligence related to the person, group or place which likely meets the law's requirements. Unlike criminal prosecutions though, the civil standard of proof generally applies meaning that the problem conduct need be proved on the balance of probabilities rather than beyond reasonable doubt. Often though, breach of any civil order issued will be a criminal offence enforceable by the criminal justice system, which has a potential "net widening" or "thinning of the mesh" effect (see Cohen, 1979, p. 346).

4.4 Moderator Analysis of How Legal Levers Impact Crime and Disorder

To test the differential effectiveness of the three forms of legal levers identified, we conducted a categorical moderator analysis using the twenty studies included in our main meta-analysis (see Section 3). We explored the different effects of the three types of legal levers: (1) code/ordinance enforcement, (2) civil action directed at both people and places, and (3) liquor licensing enforcement. Figure 11 displays the results of this analysis, where each bar represents the effect size associated with each legal lever. Effects below one (i.e., the reference line) indicate relative decreases in crime while effects above one indicate relative increases in crime. The confidence intervals for each bar represent the range of likely values for the associated effect size. Effect sizes with confidence intervals that overlap the reference line are not statistically significant, while effect sizes with confidence intervals that overlap one another do not significantly differ.

The overall results from this analysis suggest that the type of legal lever used is not a significant moderator of treatment effectiveness ($Q = 1.01$, $df = 2$, $p = 0.60$). Despite this, notable differences emerge in the estimated effect size

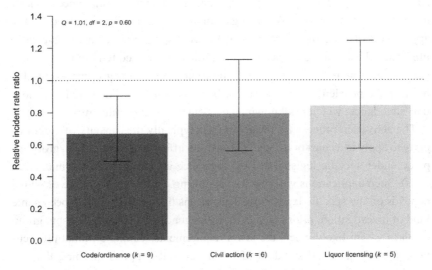

Figure 11 Moderator analysis by legal levers used.
Note: k = Number of studies, Q = The X^2 statistic of the moderator analysis.

for each legal lever. Specifically, code/ordinance enforcement is associated with an average crime decrease of 33 percent (95 percent CI: −50 percent, −10 percent), while civil action is associated with average decreases of 21 percent (95 percent CI: −44 percent, 12 percent) and liquor licensing enforcement leads to a 16 percent reduction in crime (95 percent CI: −43 percent, 24 percent). Additionally, as indicated by the confidence intervals in Figure 11, only the effect of code/ordinance enforcement is statistically significant on its own. Our moderator analysis shows, therefore, that while TPP interventions are associated with crime declines across all forms of legal levers, the effect of code/ordinance enforcement appears to be more robust based on existing evidence. Even so, it is important to note that our largest subsample of studies used code/ordinance enforcement, and that we have a relatively small number of studies overall with which to tease apart these effects.[14]

This difference in outcome effectiveness might also be explained by the fundamental differences in objectives between our three categories of legal levers. As noted above, code enforcement is typically harnessed by police to reduce specific crime problems, particularly drugs and disorder. It is often conceptualized as a police tactic. By contrast, in all but one of our liquor licensing studies, police activity was harnessed by others primarily to achieve health goals. Significantly, these liquor licensing multiagency interventions are described as reducing health harms, whereby reducing crime was not the main objective. In the civil order interventions, the overarching goal was usually described as crime prevention, alongside other intermediary objectives such as gang disruption or school attendance. Ultimately, crime reduction through these alternate mechanisms may be a longer-term goal.

4.5 Summary Comments

Our review illustrates the crucial place of legal levers in TPP interventions, which, as argued in Section 1, is a key differentiator between TPP and other policing partnership approaches. Unlike in most other partnership approaches in policing, in TPP it is the legal procedures involved in the activation of the legal lever that determines the processes of a TPP intervention. The nature of the legal lever, who (or what entity) holds it, the activation process, and the potential outcomes, all arise because of the nature of the legal frameworks available and how police engage with them. Overall, our analysis suggests that legal levers vary in their availability and suitability for specific crime problems. Police

---

[14] Note that we duplicated these analyses using RVE models. Our RVE models produced the same substantive findings as those presented here.

seeking to address crime problems need to consider their objectives, then identify which partners have levers that can help them achieve those objectives. For example, in our sample, police-led initiatives targeting problem drug places or disorder using code enforcement are likely to lead to the most direct crime reductions. As discussed earlier, these types of problem coincide with core police interests around crime and disorder, and the TPP initiatives are often coercive in nature (see Section 6) meaning that that rely on processes with which police are familiar, such as the identification of hotspots and the sanctioned use of force. What is missing from many of these studies is any analysis of the long-term outcomes and sustainability of these approaches (explored further in Section 7).

Civil orders also involve identifying problem people or places but use court orders to control behaviors. Tactics such as gang injunctions and parenting orders (for school attendance) tend to be used with problems that feature complex underlying dynamics, such as criminal sub-cultures, or social exclusion, and these are not as easily rectified as the closure of a drug house (as in a typical code enforcement example). This type of approach to crime reduction aims to disrupt deeply entrenched social patterns and this may take more time to succeed. However, we can speculate that the disruption of these patterns may lead in the long term to more sustained change than the relatively focused use of code enforcement. Similarly, benefits may be more diffuse in terms of harm reduction, community-building and health and welfare outcomes, such as those typically aimed for with the liquor licensing interventions included in our review. The number of partners involved in TPP interventions may also be significant to the achievement of these longer-term outcomes, as explored further in Section 5.

5 Optimizing the Number of Partners

One of the biggest issues in the literature on cross-sector partnerships is figuring out the optimal number of partners to involve in a cooperative venture. Babiak and Thibault (2009), in their study of Canadian sports organizations, found that "an organization is more likely to achieve its goals in a dyadic [twosome] partnership than in a partnership involving multiple organizations" (p. 136). Coulson (2005) argues that "excessive numbers of partnerships create problems of accountability and create ambiguities about who is responsible for what" (p. 155). Similarly, the challenges of multiple partners in crime control collaborations arise around sensitive data sharing, merging together of different organizational cultures, building trust among partners, and creating undue and additional administrative burdens on already busy partners (see, e.g., Mazerolle et al., 2021).

The trend to partnerships in policing stems, in part, from the global shift in the delivery of policing services away from the state as the sole provider to a plural and networked style of public security (see Crawford, 2006; Loader, 2000). The management and governance of these complex crime control collaborations is now a topic of great interest (see, e.g., Stenning & Shearing, 2018) recognizing the myriad different legislative regimes and institutional arrangements that underpin the collaborations. Indeed, Stenning and Shearing (2018) conclude that "while there have been several suggestions as to the possible architecture of the model of governance for plural policing, no such models have yet got far beyond the intellectual and aspirational drawing board anywhere in the world" (p. 57). This section takes the very specific case of TPP to assess the relative crime control benefits of policing collaborations that involve different types and numbers of partners.

5.1 Dyad versus Multiagency Partnerships

Studies were only included in our review if a partner possessed and used a specific non–criminal justice legal lever in the intervention strategy. In this section, we focus on the twenty studies included in the main meta-analysis reported in Section 3. We find that eleven (including two from Warpenius and colleagues) of the twenty TPP interventions in our review were strictly dyad – meaning two parties – partnerships (Bennett et al., 2018; Eck & Wartell, 1998; Elliott, 2007; Felson et al., 1997; Flewelling et al., 2013; Goulka et al., 2009; Holder et al., 2000; Payne, 2017; Sturgeon-Adams et al., 2005; Warpenius et al., 2010). All but one of these dyad partnership interventions were targeted at problem places (see Bennett et al., 2018 as the exception focusing on problem young people).

Nine of the twenty studies included in the meta-analysis involved more than one other partner. Three of these nine studies involved the police and three other partners, all of which brought legal levers to the partnership (Clarke & Bichler-Robertson, 1998; Koper et al., 2016; Tita et al., 2011). The Green (1996) study evaluated a TPP intervention involving four partners all possessing and using different legal levers. Five partners (all with legal levers) formed the collaborations in the Martinez (2013) and Mazerolle et al. (2000) studies. By contrast, in the Koehle (2011) study – which included five partners – only one brought a legal lever to the intervention. The Bichler et al. (2013) study involved six partners and, like the Koehle (2011) study, just one of the partners in this study possessed a legal lever. The Lurigio et al. (1998) intervention included the police working with ten partners across Cook County (Chicago), including the Cook County (Chicago) State's Attorney's Office, Chicago Health and Housing Departments, the Corporate Counsel of the City of Chicago, the Chicago Housing Court, the Cook County Recorder of Deeds, the Cook County Tax Assessor's Office, the Cook County Treasurer's Office, and the Chicago Housing Authority in the partnership. Just one of these partners – the State's Attorney's Office – possessed the legislation (the Drug Paraphernalia Act) used in the intervention.[15]

We used three approaches to test the relationship between the number of partners utilized in each TPP intervention and the associated effect on crime and disorder. First, we conducted a meta-regression including the total number of partners (including those both with and without a legal lever) in each intervention as a continuous independent variable. Second, we conducted a meta-regression including just the number of partners with a legal lever in each intervention as a continuous independent variable. Third, we constructed a measure representing the ratio of the number of partners with a legal lever to the total number of partners in the intervention and included this as a continuous independent variable in a meta-regression. The results of these analyses are presented using meta-analytic scatter/bubble plots. Each figure plots the independent variable (e.g., number of partners) on the x-axis and the estimated effect size on the y-axis. Within the plot, there is a horizontal reference or no effect line at the RIRR value of 1, the trend/prediction line for the independent variable, and point estimates for each individual study. Additionally, 95 percent confidence intervals are constructed around the trend line and the size of the individual point estimates represent the weight that each study received in the analysis (e.g., larger bubbles indicated greater weight). The hypothesized intended effect in these plots is a negative (downward) slope, as this would indicate that increases in the independent variable lead to decreasing levels of crime and disorder.

5.2 Total Number of Partners

In our first analysis across the twenty studies with an outcome measure of crime/disorder, the number of partners ranged from 1 to 10 with an average of 2.75 partners per intervention. Overall, there was a nonsignificant effect of the number of partners in each intervention on the overall preventive effects of the intervention (RIRR = 0.999, $p = 0.98$). Not only was this effect

---

[15] As an outlier intervention involving ten partners, we examine our results in this section both including and excluding the Lurigio et al. (1998) study. This study creates some positive skew in the "number of partners" measure. If the Lurigio et al. (1998) study is removed from the moderator analyses, the trend becomes more negative (i.e., more partners lead to larger crime reductions).

nonsignificant but the trend line is almost perfectly flat (see Figure 12), such that each one-unit increase in the number of partners corresponds to only a 0.1 percent additional decrease in the RIRR value (i.e., larger crime reductions). This result shows that, regardless of the total number of partners included in a TPP intervention, there is a static crime decline of approximately 25 percent for treatment groups relative to control groups. Put another way, our results suggest that there is no difference in the crime control benefits of police partnerships with one entity versus two or more entities, as the benefits are the same regardless of the total number of partners involved.

5.3 Partners with and without Legal Levers

In our second analysis we focused on the number of partners with a legal lever in each intervention. Recall that some of the interventions involved multiple partners. In these multiagency partnerships, at least one partner had to possess a legal lever to be eligible for inclusion in our review, yet sometimes the collaborations involved partners with multiple legal levers. In this analysis, we focus on the number of partners per intervention that possessed a legal lever. The number of partners with a legal lever ranged from one to five with an average of 1.85 per intervention. Interestingly, the results of our meta-regression for this measure suggest that as the number of partners with a legal lever increases, the crime reduction effect of TPP interventions may actually

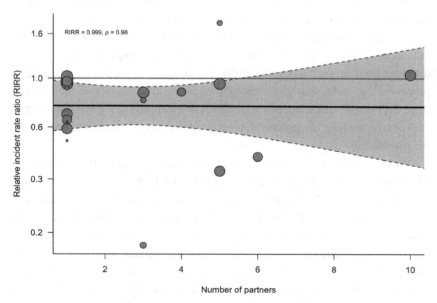

Figure 12 Meta-regression for number of partners utilized.

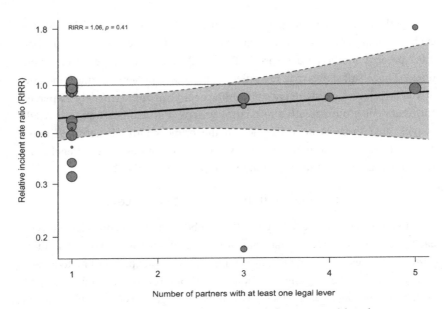

Figure 13 Meta-regression for number of partners with at least
one legal lever.

decrease (as indicated by the positive trend line in Figure 13). Specifically,
a one-unit increase in partners with a legal lever is associated with a 6 percent
increase in the RIRR value (indicating smaller reductions in crime and disorder), though this effect is not statistically significant (p = 0.41). There are
several explanations for this potential backfire effect: first, it could be that the
management and governance of these complex partnerships with entities with
different legal levers becomes embroiled in struggles around conflicting legal
processes that ultimately counteract the crime control benefits of the partnership. Second, the simultaneous application of multiple legal provisions might
stall or take too long to implement, compromising any crime control benefits of
the partnership.

Of note, one study produced findings that were discrepant from this trend.
The intervention evaluated by Clarke and Bichler-Robertson (1998) involved
three partners all with a legal lever and this study demonstrated an 83 percent
relative decrease in calls for service. Clarke and Bichler-Robertson (1998)
describe how police coerced a local slumlord who owned thirty-four residential properties to engage the services of a property management company. The
police used threats of abatement, intense media interest, and pressure
from the local business association. Taking a closer look at the Clarke and
Bichler-Robertson (1998) study, we see that the intervention partners

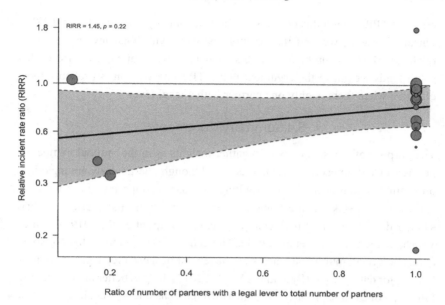

Figure 14 Meta-regression for ratio of partners with legal
level to total number of partners.

appeared to be working in a cooperative manner, but in a coercive way against the targeted slumlord (for more on this type of mixed engagement type, see Section 6). Yet while the police and partners appeared to work together in a cooperative way, the intervention involved the Building and Safety Department taking on "the lead role using standard methods to deal with code violations" (Clarke and Bichler-Robertson, 1998, p. 14). It seems, therefore, that in this particular study there emerged a clear crime control leader in the partnership that was not the police: in this case the Building and Safety Department. We further explore this idea of partner leadership later in this section.

The third and final analysis undertaken involved the construction of a measure representing the ratio of the number of partners with a legal lever to the total number of partners in the intervention (see Figure 14). This measure was included as a continuous independent variable in a meta-regression. Half of these studies comprised only one third-party partner working with police and thus generated a ratio of 1 in terms of partners with a legal lever to total partners. The average ratio was 0.87 in the number of partners with a legal lever to the total number of partners. The results of our meta-regression for this measure suggest that increases in the ratio of partners with a legal lever to the total number of partners in the intervention also lead to decreases in the preventive effect of TPP, though this effect is also not statistically significant ($p = 0.22$).[16] Put another way, we find that as more partners with legal levers are added relative to the total number of partners, there is a smaller preventive effect. This result lends weight to the argument that a TPP intervention is probably most effective when there is only one partner with a legal lever.

5.4 Summary Comments

The purpose of this section was to gather insights as to the optimal number of partners in TPP interventions. One school of thought, particularly among crime prevention practitioners, is that multiagency partnerships involving multiple entities with a stake in the crime problem are generally more effective than smaller dyad (twosome) partnerships (see, e.g., Dupont et al., 2019; Pajón & Walsh, 2023; Sedgwick et al., 2021). The general assumption is that collaborations involving multiple agencies are beneficial because they generate opportunities for data sharing (Bjelland & Vestby, 2017), help to better understand the full scope of a crime problem through a different lens (Gerassi et al., 2017), and foster trust among partners to better (and collectively) respond to problems (Bond & Gittell, 2010). And even though much is written about the difficulties of multiagency partnerships (see Berry et al., 2011), partnerships between police and just one other entity are rarely, if ever, advanced as the preferred mode for crime control (for an exception see Mazerolle, 2014).

The results from this section provide some insights as to why less might mean more in crime control partnerships, at least examined using the case of TPP partnerships. Our results show that the crime control benefits of TPP interventions are the same regardless of the total number of partners. There appear to be few (if any) crime control benefits to adding partners into a TPP crime control collaboration. Digging deeper, it appears that the problem lies with police collaborating with multiple partners that possess and bring to the collaboration different legal levers that need to follow different legal procedures. Indeed, our analysis shows that as the number of partners with a legal lever increases, the crime reduction effect of TPP interventions may actually decrease. Looking at the partnerships as a ratio of partners with legal levers to the total number of partners in the collaboration, we find that as more partners with legal levers are added to the intervention strategy relative to the total number of partners, there is less of a preventive effect. We offer here some insights as to why this might be the case.

First, in Section 4 we explored the range of legal levers used in the corpus of TPP interventions included in this Element. These different legal levers are all

---

[16] Note that we duplicated these analyses using RVE models. Our RVE models produced the same substantive findings as those presented here.

underpinned by specific procedures and processes. For example, code enforcement regulating property usage typically requires the regulator to issue a notice requiring compliance and allowing time for rectification, while civil orders like gang injunctions may be sought based on covert intelligence gathered with no prior notice to the proposed target. The activation processes, timelines, and steps involved are very different. We suggest that when different legal provisions are used simultaneously in a TPP intervention, they may be working at cross purposes. The required steps in the legal process might stall or require additional investigation. This complexity with different legal processes operating within one intervention is, we suggest, one reason why TPP interventions are likely to be most effective when there is just one partner with a legal lever. The exception to this might be a TPP intervention where one of the partners with a legal lever takes on a leadership role in the crime control effort. The Clarke and Bichler-Robertson (1998) study is a good example of the police taking a step back and leaving the leadership to a non–criminal justice agency.

Second, a large literature exists that itemizes the range of complexities and barriers that emerge in multiagency collaborations. The list of difficulties includes lack of trust between partners, mismatches between agency goals and missions, legislative restrictions on data sharing, increased burdens on frontline staff, high turnover of partnership members, cultural conflicts across different agencies, and poor understanding of the other agencies' policies and procedures. These barriers, coupled with our finding of a static crime control benefit for TPP interventions regardless of the total number of partners, beg the question as to what might motivate police (or other entities) to form multiagency partnerships to address crime problems. The seduction of inclusiveness and an all-in effort to address crime problems is profound. Yet the data do not seem to support these multiagency partnerships in their effectiveness to control crime problems.

We recognize that there may be reasons other than effectiveness to establish multiagency teams to address crime problems. Their value-add to the partnership may bring benefits such as improved access to targets, credibility, community confidence, and access to noncrime data. The amorphous and positive literature on focused deterrence is a good example of how the availability of social service assistance to target groups and individuals has facilitated reductions in violent crime committed by gangs and other criminal groups (see Braga & Weisburd, 2012). What is significant about the corpus of studies included in the review by Braga and Weisburd (2012) is that focused deterrence interventions tend to avoid the inclusion of multiple entities with different legal levers. We suggest, therefore, that the future of partnership policing needs to very carefully consider the inclusion of partners that bring non–criminal justice legal levers into the intervention strategy. More than one partner with a legal lever that sits outside of the criminal justice system may either have a backfire effect or simply result in no additional crime reduction benefits.

Overall, our conclusion concerning the optimal number of partners to involve in TPP interventions is that dyad partnerships – police partnering with just one partner that has a very clear legal lever – are likely to generate the best crime control outcomes. Police need to be trained to manage these partnerships (i.e., communication, coordination, etc.), but they do not always need to lead these partnerships (see, e.g., the Clarke & Bichler-Robertson, 1998 study).

6 Different Engagement Styles

In this section we explore how police engage with other parties in TPP interventions and the extent to which that engagement is cooperative, coercive, or a mix of the two. We situate our results within the growing interest in partnerships used to deal with many societal problems in domains such as public health, environmental protection, and urban renewal. Multifaceted crime problems similarly generate a push toward partnerships across the criminal justice system and beyond to better tackle a wide range of contemporary and highly heterogeneous crime problems. Different types of partnership are used to bring together diverse government and nongovernment parties to address these complex multifaceted problems. Some of these partnerships are highly cooperative, while others face many internal tensions. Indeed, as van Tulder and Keen (2018) note, "cross-sector partnerships face the daunting task of addressing complex societal problems by aligning different backgrounds, values, ideas and resources" (p. 315).

A distinctive feature of partnerships involving police is their capacity to use, or threaten to use, coercive legal powers to help achieve their goals. These powers can be those that are standard in the criminal justice system or powers harnessed by engaging with third parties that allow police to access their separate regulatory and private law levers (see Section 4). In TPP, threats to use these powers are often directed at the second-party targets. Elsewhere, we have described the continuum of coercive and cooperative partnerships (Mazerolle & Ransley, 2005; Mazerolle et al., 2016), and here we discuss how these elements feature in our sample of TPP studies. We draw from the systematic review results to explore any differences in the effectiveness of cooperative versus coercive partnerships in TPP interventions. While partnerships are often seen as key to tackling the multifaceted nature of entrenched crime problems, relatively little is known about their formation and engagement, what constitutes a successful partnership (Scott, 2018; van Felius et al., 2023; Webster et al., 2017), and the extent to which the nature of the engagement impacts the partnership's crime reduction objectives (Bennett et al., 2018). We examine whether the extent to which parties cooperate with or are coerced by police has any impact on outcome effectiveness.

In our third-party model (see Section 2), third-party partners are described as "proximate targets" (i.e., harnessed by police as a partner because they hold legal levers), and the criminogenic people, places, or situations are described as "ultimate targets" (see also Mazerolle & Ransley, 2005). In TPP, then, the first step is for police to secure, as a proximate target, a partner holding a legal lever. This partner is the "third party" and it is this partner that then works with police (or sometimes the third party takes the lead) to influence or control the ultimate target (the second party) and reduce criminogenic behaviors or attributes.

6.1 Classifying Different TPP Styles of Engagement

The structure of TPP interventions means that there is a formation of two distinct relationships: the first relationship is between police and the proximate, third-party target-partner (we call this the police–partner relationship) and the second is between the proximate third-party partner and the ultimate (second-party) target that has some role in the criminogenic problem (we call this the partner–target relationship). In the police–partner relationship, the partner is often a regulator. In the partner–target relationship, the engagement often exists for a noncrime control purpose, such as planning controls, building standards or safety, or alcohol or pharmacy sales. Importantly, different engagement styles can be present in both relationships. In our review, we differentiate between coercive and cooperative engagement styles in both the police–partner relationship and the partner–target relationship. By coercion we mean the involvement of an express or implied threat backed up by a sanction. By cooperation we mean a shared and mutual approach to solving a common problem (see Mazerolle & Ransley, 2005). Some TPP interventions may be coercive or cooperative in both relationships, but more commonly the police–partner relationship is largely cooperative, while the partner–target relationship varies across purely cooperative, purely coercive, or a mixture of both.

We examined the corpus of twenty-four studies to explore these different engagement styles. Our first insight is that none of our studies featured coercion in the police–partner relationship. This indicates that police approached these interventions as cooperative partnerships, and we suggest that this is most likely because the police tend to focus their energies on identifying partners who have a common interest in addressing the situation in which the crime problem exists. This does not universally mean that the partnership is easy or that the third-party partner has a direct interest in addressing the crime problem, but it does mean that the third party has some stake in the presenting situation. For example, in several of our included studies, the partnership was between police and city or state authorities responsible for health and safety (Bichler et al., 2013; Clarke & Bichler-Robertson, 1998; Eck & Wartell, 1998; Elliott, 2007; Green, 1996; Hope, 1994; Koehle, 2011; Martinez, 2013; Mazerolle et al., 2000; Morton et al., 2019; Tita et al., 2011; White et al., 2003). The legal lever and the nature of the crime problem varied, but in each case the relevant agency had its own health and safety concerns relevant to the target (e.g., unsafe properties, overcrowded housing, fire risks, community nuisance complaints). As such, both the police and their partners in these interventions had a legitimate interest in the target property or person, with the police focusing on crime and their partners focusing on health and safety. We speculate that police coercion of third-party partners is possible, but likely to arise only when that third party does not have its own interest in addressing the target or has not prioritized that interest and police pressure them to change their priorities. By contrast, as discussed in Sections 6.2–6.4, the second relationship – the partner–target relationship – varied across our intervention from cooperative to coercive, and was sometimes a mix of the two.

6.2 Cooperative Interventions

Four studies from our total of twenty-seven were classified as fully cooperative (Felson et al., 1997; Mazerolle et al., 2019; Morton et al., 2018; Sturgeon-Adams et al., 2005). We note that three of these studies provided sufficient data to calculate an effect size and were included in our moderator analysis presented in Section 6.5 (Morton et al., 2018 was excluded, as discussed in Section 3). The four fully cooperative interventions included examples of all three types of legal lever discussed in Section 4 (i.e., code or ordinance enforcement, civil orders to control behavior, and liquor licensing). In one of the code enforcement studies, police partnered with fire and emergency services to engage hotel operators to control the use of their properties for drug offending (Morton et al., 2018). Hotel operators in the treatment group received a letter educating them about drug-related harms in and around hotels and encouraging them to report suspicious behaviors. This was followed by a visit by police and partner agencies, to cultivate them as intelligence sources and engage their cooperation. While partner agencies would have held some enforcement levers, the study does not describe them as being used or threatened. Instead, the goal was to engage the ultimate targets as crime control partners and informants (Morton et al., 2018).

The civil order cases featuring fully cooperative engagement styles also relied on recruiting targets as voluntary participants. One involved a partnership between police and schools to target truancy, as a precursor to youth crime (Mazerolle et al., 2019). The mechanism to achieve this was a procedurally just dialogue scripted into school and police meetings with truanting young people and their guardians to communicate the legislative responsibilities of parents to have their children attend school. While a legal lever existed, in the form of schools' powers to issue violation notices to parents, the study reports a concerted effort to not escalate the case through the regulatory pyramid and steer away from the use of coercion. Similarly, the other civil order case involved community collaboration with police and other agencies to alley-gate a laneway which was the site for crime (Sturgeon-Adams et al., 2005), with no evidence of any coercion in the study. Interestingly, of the four fully cooperative partnerships, three seemed to have involved researchers or non-police analysts in the design stage (Mazerolle et al., 2019; Morton et al., 2018; Sturgeon-Adams et al., 2005). Although the number of studies is small, this may suggest that TPP interventions that are co-developed with police and researchers may be more likely to feature collaboration, seeking to move away from reliance on force and sanction use.

Felson and colleagues (1997) also describe a cooperative partnership and in this study the intervention aimed to tackle alcohol-related crime and disorder. The lever-holding third party was a liquor licensing authority, which could impose license restrictions on venues. The ultimate targets were bar operators, whose business practices could promote problem drinking (e.g., noncompliance with regulations on underage drinking, responsible service, service practices that promoted excessive drinking). The police and the licensing authority worked cooperatively with bar operators to develop and implement a voluntary accord governing the movement of patrons, given that bar-hopping and excessive patron congregation could lead to crime. The accord was directed at meeting the regulator's goals of controlling service environments, as well as police goals around crime reduction. While largely relying on cooperation from bar operators, there was an implied sanction or "hidden stick" (Felson et al., 1997, p. 126) in that the licensing authority could investigate and close down noncompliant operators or deny requests for expanded operations. Yet this "stick" was never articulated in the intervention or ever used.

6.3 Coercive Interventions

Our studies reveal that coercive elements in the partner–target relationship were common in the majority of our TPP interventions. Coercion featured in interventions where the legal lever was code or ordinance enforcement, civil orders to control behavior, and liquor licensing enforcement. One study (Mazerolle et al., 2000) involved police partnering with city regulators to use the threat of code citations against problem landlords seen to be allowing drug crime on their properties. The threat was often enforced, with the study reporting that "about two thirds of the targeted sites are cited for at least one code violation from a city inspector" (Mazerolle et al., 2000, p. 216). The two studies targeting pharmacy sales of drug precursors (Ferris et al., 2016; Hattingh et al., 2016) were coercive because the legal lever of mandatory recording and reporting of sales was imposed by legislation, breach of which attracted fines, potential professional discipline, and potential criminal action.

An example of a coercive study (in the partner–target aspect of the TPP relationship) featuring a civil order to control behavior involved police partnering with other law enforcement and city authorities to target landlords who owned properties where gun crime was prevalent (Koper et al., 2016). The use of civil nuisance orders accompanied a criminal justice "crackdown," and, while there were some cooperative elements with relevant communities, the intervention is described primarily in terms of the nuisance order, with outcomes reported including summonses, citations, and properties being condemned (Koper et al., 2016, p. 127). Similarly, a coercive liquor licensing intervention was featured in one study where police and licensing authorities targeted liquor retailers to enforce underage drinking laws (Flewelling et al., 2013). The study describes as "a substantial component of the project" enforcement of compliance checks of retailers across the intervention communities (Flewelling et al., 2013, p. 267) with the lever being license sanctions.

We speculate that these coercive engagement interventions are less likely to succeed in the long run (see Mazerolle, 2014) because these types of intervention are unlikely to change the underlying dynamics of the ultimate targets. Bichler and colleagues (2013) provide some insights as to why these underlying motivations might not change. In this study, police identified budget motels as sites with high levels of crime problems. Six city agencies (including the City Attorney as well as finance, fire, police, planning and building, and community development) formed a working group that developed an "annual permit process that used compliance with public safety standards to issue permits to operate motels" (Bichler et al., 2013, p. 445). The city agencies collectively constituted the third-party partners, who could use the permit process as a lever to address criminogenic behaviors of the ultimate targets, the motel operators, who could in turn influence crime-promoting activities at their premises. The relationship between the police and the third parties was described as a cooperative problem-solving initiative. But Bichler and colleagues (2013) reported the coercive nature of the engagement with moteliers specifically by both the police and the third parties where police worked with the other agencies to shame the managers and owners into taking crime control action, "distributing reports to motel operators that ranked each motel property by calls for service per room rate from highest to lowest" (p. 445). This shaming was reinforced by the fact that the permit to operate could be revoked if calls for service exceeded stipulated limits.

The central concept of shaming is well understood in criminology (see Braithwaite, 1989) and the application of disintegrative shaming – as reported in the way the police use shame in the Bichler and colleagues (2013) study – is known to lead to labeling, stigmatization, ostracism, and an increase rather than a decrease in a range of different types of offending (Ahmed et al., 2001; McAlinden, 2006). We argue that this type of shaming, coercive engagement style used by the police and third parties to coopt the second parties/ultimate targets is unlikely to change the long-term motivations of the motel owners. Notably, the outcome measure in this study was reduced calls for police service, rather than reduced crime and disorder or reduced fear of crime. Reduced calls for police service is an outcome that is wholly serving the police agency. The Bichler and colleagues (2013) study does not report whether this outcome met the goals of the third parties (who may have been more concerned with health and safety outcomes). The extent to which this intervention engagement style is, at best, silent on involving shared goals and, at worst, dominated by those of one partner at the expense of the other is likely to affect long-term partnership sustainability (van Felius et al., 2023). This type of coercive TPP intervention, therefore, is likely to fail for two reasons: shaming the motel owners is unlikely to change their long-term behaviors and a mismatch of intervention goals between the partners is likely to cause tensions in the partnership in the long run.

6.4 Mixed Engagement Styles

Mixed engagement approaches are defined in this review when interventions against the target involve both coercive and cooperative elements. The TPP interventions we classified as mixed (four of which provided sufficient data for the moderator analysis presented in Section 6.5), featured either code/ordinance enforcement or liquor licensing. No studies featuring civil orders were found in this category. In Hope's (1994) study, police partnered in separate instances with city regulators and a finance company to influence property owners to address drug problems at their properties. Hope (1994) describes the cooperative elements as group meetings with property owners in intervention areas and visits to targeted properties to persuade owners to take action, and the coercive elements as code citations and leveraging the finance company to threaten foreclosure over one of the properties.

Payne (2017), in another mixed engagement style study, explained initiatives in Anchorage (Alaska) and Green Bay (Wisconsin) that involved police notices called "notice of potential future fines" being sent to property owners (p. 926): these notices activated ordinances created by the local authority and threatened property owners with fines if nuisance activity continued for more than fifteen days after the chronic nuisance notification was issued and if the property owner had not made reasonable efforts to abate the nuisance.

The mixed interventions involving liquor licensing all accompanied enforcement activities with programs of education and/or community engagement. For example, Warpenius and colleagues (2010) describe two multi-component interventions in Finland targeting the serving of alcohol to intoxicated drinkers. This is described as including several parallel, coordinated actions specifically designed as a multi-component approach and including information campaigns, training, and community mobilization, accompanied by enforcement activity and strengthened structures for cooperation among relevant agencies.

Another example of a mixed TPP relationship involved an intervention to address crime and disorder problems generated by properties owned by slum landlords (Clarke & Bichler-Robertson, 1998). Police activated city agency officers (building, safety, and fire departments and the City Attorney) as partners who could exert pressure on landlords to clean up their properties and better govern their tenants (via stricter tenancy rules and screening, access restrictions, higher security deposits, prompt evictions, and hiring of property managers). In this case, the lever-holding third parties were the city agencies that possessed powers and sanctions under their regulatory codes, and the ultimate targets were the landlords who could influence how their properties were used, so as to reduce the presence of criminogenic tenants. The relationship between the police and the city authorities appears to have been cooperative: they shared a common goal of cleaning up poorly managed sites, which met health and safety objectives as well as improving crime control. Yet the relationship between the city authorities and the slum landlords oscillated between cooperation and coercive elements: initial efforts by the city authorities aimed to persuade the landlords to take remedial action, but, if this failed, city authorities used their powers to initiate coercive code violation processes.

6.5 Moderator Analysis to Assess the Impact of Engagement Styles

We conducted a categorical moderator analysis to test how these different engagement styles impacted crime and disorder outcomes across the twenty studies included in our main meta-analysis. We explored the differential effects

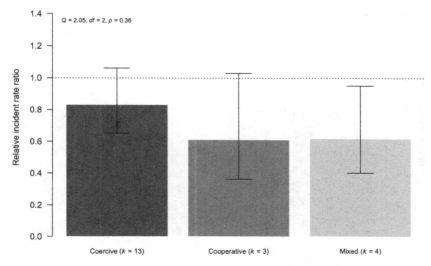

Figure 15 Moderator analysis for engagement type.
Note: k = Number of studies, Q = The X^2 statistic of the moderator analysis.

of three types of partnership: (1) thirteen coercive interventions, (2) three fully cooperative interventions, and (3) four mixed engagement style interventions. Figure 15 displays the results of this analysis, where each bar represents the effect size associated with each category.

As shown in Figure 15, the results from this analysis suggest that the type of partnership used in the TPP intervention is not a significant moderator of treatment effectiveness (Q = 2.05, df = 2, p = 0.36). Despite this, both fully cooperative and mixed partnerships display notably larger effect sizes than coercive partnerships. While coercive partnerships are associated with an average relative crime decline of approximately 17 percent (95 percent CI: −35 percent, 6 percent), cooperative and mixed partnerships are associated with average relative declines of 39 percent (95 percent CI: −64 percent, 3 percent) and 38 percent (95 percent CI: −60 percent, −5 percent), respectively. Only the effect of mixed partnerships, however, is statistically significant individually.

We also tested this relationship as a dichotomy, combining fully cooperative and mixed partnerships into a single category because in all of our studies the mixed nature of the engagement style involved collaboration between police and their third-party partners. The results of this analysis can be seen in Figure 16. Once again, while not statistically significant (Q = 2.13, df = 1, p = 0.14), interventions involving cooperative elements between police and their third-party partners were associated with considerably larger effect sizes than interventions relying solely on coercive partnerships. Cooperative and mixed

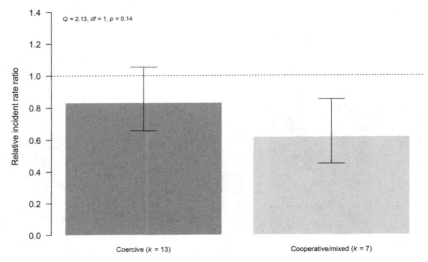

Figure 16 Moderator analysis for engagement type (dichotomous).
Note: k = Number of studies, Q = The X^2 statistic of the moderator analysis.

partnerships were associated with average relative crime declines of approximately 38 percent (95 percent CI: −55 percent, −15 percent), while coercive partnerships were associated with average relative declines of 17 percent (95 percent CI: −34 percent, 5 percent). Additionally, the crime reduction effect of cooperative and mixed partnerships was statistically significant on its own, while the effect of coercive partnerships was not.[17]

6.6 Summary Comments

Looking across the studies included in our systematic review, coercion was clearly the dominant engagement style in the third-party partner–target relationship. The tools of coercion were the communication of legal powers held by the third party and warnings about the consequences if they were used. In the fully cooperative engagement style studies and the cooperative elements in the police–third-party partner relationship, we identified a range of features that are found to be characteristics of cross-sector partnerships in the literature more generally (see Clarke & Crane, 2018). For example, several studies described the importance of communication through regular meetings (see Eck & Wartell, 1998; Elliott, 2007; Koehle, 2011; Martinez, 2013; Warpenius & Holmila, 2008), reliable follow-up, and "working with" (rather than against) third-party

---

[17] Note that we duplicated these analyses using RVE models. Our RVE models produced the same substantive findings as those presented here.

targets (like apartment managers) in police efforts to cooperatively reduce serious crime problems. Ferris and colleagues (2016) described how police sometimes engaged with pharmacists to support mandatory recording of PSE product sales by helping them to better identify suspicious requests for PSE products.

The use of coercion or cooperative engagement does not appear to be related to any specific crime problem or type of legal lever. Instead, the nature of the engagement appears to be a conscious choice of either the police or the third parties (or both working together). That is, we suggest that the police and their partners choose how to engage with their ultimate targets. The fact that coercion is often the chosen mode of engagement may indicate that this is the framework most familiar to police. It may be the case that the effort and skills needed for genuine cooperation with the targets of crime control take more time. In a world of time-poor policing, it may be quicker and easier for police to use threats of citations or civil orders than to take the time to foster a willingness to comply. The fact that there are cooperative engagement elements across many of our studies indicates that there are better ways to approach crime reduction if the police choose to engage in them, and some of those ways are also more likely to be fair and procedurally just.

We note that some of these fully cooperative styles of engagement involve co-designed interventions with researchers (see Mazerolle et al., 2019; Morton et al., 2018; Sturgeon-Adams et al., 2005). These co-designed interventions specifically activated the key principles of procedural justice policing, with specific efforts to motivate ultimate second-party targets to comply in the first stages of engagement. Mazerolle and colleagues (2016) show how, in the responsive regulatory model, the ultimate target can be coaxed into compliance through procedurally fair communication focusing on how deterrent-based sanctions could be activated further up the pyramid. Braithwaite (2011) explains that voluntary compliance can be fostered in the vast majority of situations, preserving perceptions of legitimacy pertaining to the law or the regulator, if the regulatory process begins with procedurally fair dialogue involving counseling, education, and awareness before proceeding with legal measures.

The key lesson for those considering TPP as a response to crime and disorder problems is that the evidence suggests more pronounced effects of successful outcomes when some degree of collaboration is involved with the crime control targets. As discussed, in most circumstances the police and their partners have flexibility and choice in how they choose to engage, and our analysis suggests that, where possible, that choice should favor cooperative approaches.

7 Conclusion

Our review draws from a corpus of experimental and quasi-experimental studies to assess the effectiveness of TPP interventions gathered using a systematic search and screening process. Calculating effect sizes that compare the pre- to post-intervention change in crime and disorder for treatment groups to the pre- to post-intervention change in crime and disorder for control groups, we find that TPP interventions are associated with a statistically significant 25 percent decline in crime and disorder. These crime control outcomes demonstrate evidence of a diffusion of crime control benefits rather than a spatial displacement effect. Our results also show that TPP interventions targeting microgeographic areas are associated with larger crime reductions than interventions targeting macrogeographic areas and that the strongest deterrent effect of TPP can be found when targeting drug/disorder offenses and the weakest deterrent effect is on violent offenses.

Beyond the overall effectiveness of TPP interventions, we conducted moderator analyses to explore some of the nuances of TPP, focusing on how different legal levers, numbers of partners, and engagement styles shaped the relative effectiveness of TPP interventions. We found that code enforcement and dyad (twosome) partnerships using cooperative engagement styles are associated with more crime control benefits than TPP interventions using civil actions or orders and liquor licensing enforcement that involve multiple partners and sometimes coercive engagement styles. We offer some theoretical and practical insights around these findings.

The growth in the regulatory state during the 1980s and 1990s created new and exciting opportunities for police to foster partnerships with a range of nodes, entities, and agencies (Mazerolle & Ransley, 2006). The original identification of TPP (see Buerger & Mazerolle, 1998; Green, 1996) occurred right at the height of this global transformation in governance. Many other types of police partnership also emerged in the late 1980s and 1990s, including community policing and POP, with partnerships taking many different forms: some were complex, multiagency partnerships (such as Lurigio et al., 1998); others relied upon community organizations as their primary partners (see Tita et al., 2011); and other variations of partnership policing focused exclusively on just one other partner (see Mazerolle et al., 2019). Multiagency and partnership approaches accelerated further in the 2000s, driven by post–global financial crisis austerity in many police budgets (Millie & Bullock, 2013; Topping, 2022) just as the police were expected to do more in both crime prevention and social welfare, such as dealing with mental illness in the community (Millie, 2013). Meanwhile, cross-agency intelligence failures (such as in preventing terrorism) further intensified widespread adoption of multiagency approaches in policing partnerships.

Fast forward to 2024 and we suggest that there is now an established expectation of partnership approaches in policing (Howe, 2019; Makin & Marenin, 2017; Sedgwick et al., 2021). This expectation that the police can and will do better when they partner with other entities to control crime and disorder problems poses both opportunities and challenges. The opportunities are demonstrated in the results of our review: we show the clear crime control benefits the police can achieve when they work in partnership with third-party partners. Yet the challenges in partnership policing pose some real questions for the future of TPP. First, we recognize the intuitive appeal of the "all-in" multiagency approach. Many agencies working together can bring different data and intelligence to intractable problems, offer wraparound services for complex crime-involved individual people or problem places, and share scarce resources to efficiently tackle contemporary problems. Yet our results presented in this Element find that there is no difference in the crime control benefits of partnerships between the police and one, two, or more entities. Moreover, we find that as the number of partners with a legal lever increases, the crime reduction effect of TPP interventions decreases. We have offered several reasons for why we find this result, focusing on the lack of cross-sector, cross-agency trust and the difficulties police face when trying to manage these complex multiagency partnerships. We hypothesize that multi-partner interventions in TPP might be complicated by the different activation processes involved in accessing the partners' legal levers, which add complexity to the management of such interventions. Further, these approaches are likely to take more police time and effort to manage as the number of partners increases. We conclude, therefore, that police may want to focus in the future on fostering dyad, third-party partnerships and accessing other multiple agencies on an "as needed" basis.

The second challenge in partnership policing – and TPP partnerships in particular – is working out ways to use cooperative rather than coercive engagement styles, particularly in engaging with what we refer to as the second-party, ultimate targets. Here, the theory of responsive regulation (see Braithwaite, 2011) provides some important insights. Our review of TPP in this Element finds that partners that bring a code enforcement legal lever to the intervention are more effective in controlling crime and disorder problems than partners that offer access to civil orders. Unlike civil orders, both code and liquor enforcement often follow the incentivized model of responsive regulation. The responsive regulatory pyramid (Ayres & Braithwaite, 1992) illustrates the way that regulators use their discretion to consistently respond to breaches via counseling and education, then warnings, and only escalating cases to the point of formal sanctions when the targets of the orders fail to rectify the problems. Cooperative styles of engagement with incentives to engage with the ultimate targets in TPP initiatives are shown to be effective and offer most promise in TPP interventions. By contrast, civil orders such as gang or nuisance injunctions generally do not incentivize offenders to cooperate, relying instead on incapacitation, disruption, or deterrence. To activate these powers, police or partners gather evidence about a person's activity or activities in a particular place or area. The evidence required usually need only meet a civil standard of proof rather than a criminal one because the order is civil in nature. We find, furthermore, that TPP interventions using civil orders are less effective than those using code enforcement. It should be noted, however, that the technique is more likely to be directed at longer-term disruption rather than shorter-term crime control, which may partly explain these results. We note that it is possible for civil orders to be applied in ways that are likely to garner willing cooperation and show effectiveness over time (Braga & Weisburd, 2012). In focused deterrence, for example, the police and their partners cooperatively communicate and seek to resolve serious gang and violent crime problems with gang members. A warning, for example, is not necessarily required under a civil order. Yet the manner in which gang members are "warned" in focused deterrence interventions adds in elements of responsive regulation that are an important ingredient in the success of focused deterrence interventions. Hence, civil orders are more likely to be effective when used as part of a suite of measures, as in focused deterrence, rather than on their own.

The third challenge in TPP interventions is working out ways to sustain the crime control gains that the immediate intervention provides; TPP is characterized by a shift in responsibility for the crime or disorder problem from the police to the third party. Yet we see a wide range of ways in which this shift in responsibility actually occurs in our corpus of studies: in some TPP interventions, the third party assumes the lead role in the intervention almost immediately and the legal processes of the third party dictates the intervention from the outset (see Bichler et al., 2013). In other TPP interventions, the police push and prod the third party to act according to their laws, sometimes being successful in getting the third parties to act in a sustained manner (see Green, 1996; Mazerolle et al., 2000) and sometimes not (see Morton et al., 2018). For TPP to foster a sustainable partnership, the police need a partner with a legal lever (preferably a regulatory lever) that can be applied in a procedurally fair, consistent manner and where the partner's organization equally benefits from applying the law. We see this type of sustainable partnership in the Ability School Engagement Program (ASEP) that targeted truanting young people who were already known to police (Mazerolle et al., 2019). In ASEP, both the police and the schools benefited from the application of the truancy laws, and communication of the legal obligations of the parents was undertaken in a structured, procedurally fair manner.

In conclusion, this Element offers several practical guidelines for police. We suggest that the police choose their crime control partners very carefully, considering the specificity of the role that each partner can bring to the table. Often, this will mean focusing efforts to forge dyad partnerships (police with just one partner) with agencies or entities with a code enforcement–style legal lever. While activation of the third party's lever must follow the legislated processes, this should be layered in the context of procedurally fair engagement. When police deliberately use a cooperative engagement style with both third-party partners and ultimate, second-party targets, they are more likely to foster a greater willingness to cooperate and nurture the chances of sustaining the crime control gains.

References

Addington, L. A. (2009). *Measuring Crime*. Oxford Bibliographies Online Research Guide. https://doi.org/10.1093/obo/9780195396607-0057.

Ahmed, E., Harris, N., Braithwaite, J., & Braithwaite, V. (2001). *Shame Management Through Reintegration*. Cambridge Studies in Criminology. Cambridge: Cambridge University Press.

Andrews, T. (2023). Co-operation or unification: Is the future of police multi-agency working simply to become one agency? *Police Journal, 96* (3), 451–470. https://doi.org/10.1177/0032258x221094494.

Anzures-Cabrera, J., & Higgins, J. P. T. (2010). Graphical displays for meta-analysis: An overview with suggestions for practice. *Research Synthesis Methods, 1*(1), 66–80. https://doi.org/10.1002/jrsm.6.

Ayling, J. (2013). Harnessing third parties for transnational environmental crime prevention. *Transnational Environmental Law, 2*(2), 339–362. https://doi.org/10.1017/S2047102513000174.

Ayling, J., & Grabosky, P. (2006). When police go shopping. *Policing: An International Journal of Police Strategies and Management, 29*(4), 665–690. https://doi.org/10.1108/13639510610711592.

Ayres, I., & Braithwaite, J. (1992). *Responsive Regulation: Transcending the Deregulation Debate*. New York: Oxford University Press.

Babiak, K., & Thibault, L. (2009). Challenges in multiple cross-sector partnerships. *Nonprofit and Voluntary Sector Quarterly, 38*(1), 117–143. https://doi.org/10.1177/0899764008316054.

Bayley, D. H. (1994). *Police for the Future*. New York: Oxford University Press.

Bayley, D. H. (2016). The complexities of 21st century policing. *Policing: A Journal of Policy and Practice, 10*(3), 163–170. https://doi.org/10.1093/police/paw019.

Bayley, D. H., & Shearing, C. D. (2001). *The New Structure of Policing: Description, Conceptualization, and Research Agenda*. Washington, DC: National Institute of Justice. https://babel.hathitrust.org/cgi/pt?id=mdp.39015054163772&seq=3.

Bennett, S., Mazerolle, L., Antrobus, E., Eggins, E., & Piquero, A. R. (2018). Truancy intervention reduces crime: Results from a randomized field trial. *Justice Quarterly, 35*(2), 309–329. https://doi.org/10.1080/07418825.2017.1313440.

* Asterisk denotes studies included in the review.

Bennett, T. (1991). The effectiveness of a police-initiated fear-reducing strategy. *British Journal of Criminology*, *31*(1), 1–14. https://doi.org/10.1093/oxfordjournals.bjc.a048075.

Berry, G., Briggs, P., Erol, R., & van Staden, L. (2011). *The Effectiveness of Partnership Working in a Crime and Disorder Context: A Rapid Evidence Assessment*. Research Report 52. London: Home Office. https://shorturl.at/5egFo.

*Bichler, G., Schmerler, K., & Enriquez, J. (2013). Curbing nuisance motels: An evaluation of police as place regulators. *Policing: An International Journal of Police Strategies and Management*, *36*(2), 437–462. https://doi.org/10.1108/13639511311329787.

Bjelland, H. F., & Vestby, A. (2017). "It's about using the full sanction catalogue": On boundary negotiations in a multi-agency organised crime investigation. *Policing and Society*, *27*(6), 655–670. https://doi.org/10.1080/10439463.2017.1341510.

Bond, B. J., & Gittell, J. H. (2010). Cross-agency coordination of offender reentry: Testing collaboration outcomes. *Journal of Criminal Justice*, *38*(2), 118–129. https://doi.org/10.1016/j.jcrimjus.2010.02.003.

Borenstein, M., Hedges, L. V., Higgins, J. P. T., & Rothstein, H. R. (2009). *Introduction to Meta-analysis*. Chichester: John Wiley & Sons.

Borenstein, M., Hedges, L. V., Higgins, J. P. T., & Rothstein, H. R. (2010). A basic introduction to fixed-effect and random-effects models for meta-analysis. *Research Synthesis Methods*, *1*(2), 97–111. https://doi.org/10.1002/jrsm.12.

Braga, A. A. (2008). Pulling levers focused deterrence strategies and the prevention of gun homicide. *Journal of Criminal Justice*, *36*(4), 332–343. https://doi.org/10.1016/j.jcrimjus.2008.06.009.

Braga, A. A., & Weisburd, D. (2006). Critic – Problem-oriented policing: The disconnect between principles and practice. In D. Weisburd & A. A. Braga (eds.), *Police Innovation: Contrasting Perspectives*, 2nd ed. (pp. 133–152). Cambridge: Cambridge University Press.

Braga, A. A., & Weisburd, D. L. (2012). The effects of "pulling levers" focused deterrence strategies on crime. *Campbell Systematic Reviews*, *8*(1), 1–90. https://doi.org/10.4073/csr.2012.6.

Braga, A. A., Turchan, B., Papachristos, A. V., & Hureau, D. M. (2019a). Hot spots policing of small geographic areas effects on crime. *Campbell Systematic Reviews*, *15*(3), e1046. https://doi.org/10.1002/cl2.1046.

Braga, A. A., Turchan, B., & Winship, C. (2019b). Critic – Partnership, accountability, and innovation: Clarifying Boston's experience with focused deterrence.

In D. Weisburd & A. A. Braga (eds.), *Police Innovation: Contrasting Perspectives*, 2nd ed. (pp. 227–247). Cambridge: Cambridge University Press.

Braithwaite, J. (1989). *Crime, Shame and Reintegration*. Cambridge: Cambridge University Press.

Braithwaite, J. (2000). The new regulatory state and the transformation of criminology. *British Journal of Criminology*, *40*(2), 222–238. https://doi .org/10.1093/bjc/40.2.222.

Braithwaite, J. (2006). Responsive regulation and developing economies. *World Development*, *34*(5), 884–898. https://doi.org/10.1016/j.worlddev .2005.04.021.

Braithwaite, J. (2011). Fasken lecture: The essence of responsive regulation. *University of British Columbia Law Review*, *44*(3), 475–520.

Brodeur, J. P. ([2008] 2014). Scientific policing and criminal investigation. In S. Leman-Langlois (ed.), *Technocrime: Technology, Crime and Social Control* (pp. 169–193). Abingdon: Routledge.

Buerger, M. E., & Mazerolle, L. (1998). Third-party policing: A theoretical analysis of an emerging trend. *Justice Quarterly*, *15*(2), 301–327. https://doi .org/10.1080/07418829800093761.

Bullock, K. (2013). Community, intelligence-led policing and crime control. *Policing and Society*, *23*(2), 125–144. https://doi.org/10.1080/10439463 .2012.671822.

Cartwright, N. (2007). Are RCTs the gold standard? *BioSocieties*, *2*(1), 11–20. https://doi.org/10.1017/S1745855207005029.

Cheh, M. (1998). Civil remedies to control crime: Legal issues and constitutional challenges. *Crime Prevention Studies*, *9*, 45–66.

Clarke, A., & Crane, A. (2018). Cross-sector partnerships for systemic change: Systematized literature review and agenda for further research. *Journal of Business Ethics*, *150*(2), 303–313. https://doi.org/10.1007/s10551-018-3922-2.

Clarke, R. V. (2009). Situational crime prevention: Theoretical background and current practice. In M. D. Krohn, A. J. Lizotte, & G. P. Hall (eds.), *Handbook on Crime and Deviance* (pp. 259–276). New York: Springer.

*Clarke, R. V., & Bichler-Robertson, G. (1998). Place managers, slumlords and crime in low rent apartment buildings. *Security Journal*, *11*(1), 11–19.

Clarke, R. V., & Newman, G. R. (2007). Police and the prevention of terrorism. *Policing: A Journal of Policy and Practice*, *1*(1), 9–20. https://doi.org/ 10.1093/police/pam003.

Cohen, J. (1988). *Statistical Power Analysis for the Behavioral Sciences*, 2nd ed. New York: Lawrence Erlbaum Associates.

Cohen, L. E., & Felson, M. (1979). Social change and crime rate trends: A routine activity approach. *American Sociological Review, 44*(4), 588–608. https://doi .org/10.2307/2094589.

Cohen, S. (1979). The punitive city: Notes on the dispersal of social control. *Contemporary Crises, 3*(4), 339–363. https://doi.org/10.1007/BF00729115.

Cook, T. D., & Campbell, D. T. (1979). *Quasi-experimentation: Design and Analysis Issues for Field Settings*. Boston, MA: Houghton Mifflin.

Cornish, D. B., & Clarke, R. V. (2003). Opportunities, precipitators and criminal decisions: A reply to Wortley's critique of situational crime prevention. *Crime Prevention Studies, 16*, 41–96.

Corsaro, N., Brunson, R. K., & McGarrell, E. F. (2013). Problem-oriented policing and open-air drug markets: Examining the Rockford pulling levers deterrence strategy. *Crime and Delinquency, 59*(7), 1085–1107. https://doi .org/10.1177/0011128709345955.

Coulson, A. (2005). A plague on all your partnerships: Theory and practice in regeneration. *International Journal of Public Sector Management, 18*(2), 151–163. https://doi.org/10.1108/09513550510584973.

Crawford, A. (2006). Networked governance and the post-regulatory state? Steering, rowing and anchoring the provision of policing and security. *Theoretical Criminology, 10*(4), 449–479. https://doi.org/10.1177/ 1362480606068874.

Crawford, A., & Evans, K. (2017). Crime prevention and community safety. In A. Liebling, S. Maruna, & L. McAra (eds.), *The Oxford Handbook of Criminology*, 6th ed. (pp. 797–824). Oxford: Oxford University Press.

Dupont, B., Whelan, C., & Manning, P. K. (2019). *Policing Across Organisational Boundaries: Developments in Theory and Practice*. New York: Routledge.

Duval, S., & Tweedie, R. (2000). A nonparametric "trim and fill" method of accounting for publication bias in meta-analysis. *Journal of the American Statistical Association, 95*(449), 89–98. https://doi.org/10.2307/2669529.

Eck, J. E. (1994). *Drug Markets and Drug Places: A Case-Control Study of the Spatial Structure of Illicit Drug Dealing*. PhD thesis, University of Maryland, College Park. www.proquest.com/docview/304097846.

Eck, J. E. (2003). Police problems: The complexity of problem theory, research and evaluation. *Crime Prevention Studies, 15*, 79–114.

Eck, J. E. (2019). Place managers and crime places. *Oxford Research Encyclopedia of Criminology and Criminal Justice*. https://doi.org/10.1093/ acrefore/9780190264079.013.307.

Eck, J. E., & Spelman, W. (1987). Who ya gonna call? The police as problem-busters. *Crime and Delinquency, 33*(1), 31–52. https://doi.org/ 10.1177/0011128787033001003.

*Eck, J. E., & Wartell, J. (1998). Improving the management of rental properties with drug problems: A randomized experiment. In L. Mazerolle & J. Roehl (eds.), *Civil Remedies and Crime Prevention*. Crime Prevention Studies, vol. 9 (pp. 161–186). Monsey, NY: Criminal Justice Press.

Egger, M., Smith, G. D., Schneider, M., & Minder, C. (1997). Bias in meta-analysis detected by a simple, graphical test. *British Medical Journal*, *315*(7109), 629–634. https://doi.org/10.1136/bmj.315.7109.629.

*Elliott, M. (2007). *An Evaluation of Specialized Police Response Teams on Motel Crime*. MA thesis. University of Nevada, Reno. www.proquest.com/docview/304827949.

Ericson, R. V., & Haggerty, K. D. (1997). *Policing the Risk Society*. Toronto: University of Toronto Press.

Farrington, D. P. (2003). Methodological quality standards for evaluation research. *Annals of the American Academy of Political and Social Science*, *587*(1), 49–68. https://doi.org/10.1177/0002716202250789.

Farrington, D. P., & Welsh, B. C. (2002). *Effects of Improved Street Lighting on Crime: A Systematic Review*. Home Office Research Study 251. London: Home Office. https://shorturl.at/6xMT6.

Farrington, D. P., & Welsh, B. C. (2009). *Making Public Places Safer: Surveillance and Crime Prevention*. New York: Oxford University Press.

Felson, M. (1995). Those who discourage crime. In J. E. Eck & D. Weisburd (eds.), *Crime and Place*. Crime Prevention Studies, vol. 4 (pp. 53–66). Monsey, NY: Criminal Justice Press and Police Executive Research Forum.

*Felson, M., Berends, R., Richardson, B., & Veno, A. E. (1997). Reducing pub hopping and related crime. In R. Homel (ed.), *Policing for Prevention: Reducing Crime, Public Intoxication and Injury*. Crime Prevention Studies, vol. 7 (pp. 115–132). Monsey, NY: Criminal Justice Press.

*Ferris, J., Devaney, M., Mazerolle, L., & Sparkes-Carroll, M. (2016). *Assessing the Utility of Project STOP in Reducing Pseudoephedrine Diversion to Clandestine Laboratories*. Trends and Issues in Crime and Criminal Justice, vol. 509 (pp. 1–7). Canberra, ACT: Australian Institute of Criminology. https://doi.org/10.52922/ti235944.

Fisher, Z., & Tipton, E. (2015). robumeta: An R-package for robust variance estimation in meta-analysis. *arXiv*. https://doi.org/10.48550/arXiv.1503.02220.

Fleming, J. (2006). Working through networks: The challenge of partnership policing. In J. Wood, J. Fleming, & J. D. Wood (eds.), *Fighting Crime Together: The Challenges of Policing and Security Networks* (pp. 87–115). Sydney: University of New South Wales Press.

*Flewelling, R. L., Grube, J. W., Paschall, M. J., Biglan, A., Kraft, A., Black, C., Hanley, S. M., Ringwalt, C., Wiesen, C., & Ruscoe, J. (2013). Reducing youth access to alcohol: Findings from a community-based randomized trial. *American Journal of Community Psychology*, *51*(1–2), 264–277. https://doi.org/10.1007/s10464-012-9529-3.

Garland, D. (2002). *The Culture of Control: Crime and Social Order in Contemporary Society*. Oxford: Oxford University Press.

Gerassi, L., Nichols, A., & Michelson, E. (2017). Lessons learned: Benefits and challenges in interagency coalitions addressing sex trafficking and commercial sexual exploitation. *Journal of Human Trafficking*, *3*(4), 285–302. https://doi.org/10.1080/23322705.2016.1260345.

Gill, C., Weisburd, D., Telep, C. W., Vitter, Z., & Bennett, T. (2014). Community-oriented policing to reduce crime, disorder and fear and increase satisfaction and legitimacy among citizens: A systematic review. *Journal of Experimental Criminology*, *10*(4), 399–428. https://doi.org/10.1007/s11292-014-9210-y.

Goldkamp, J. S., & Vîlcică, E. R. (2008). Targeted enforcement and adverse system side effects: The generation of fugitives in Philadelphia. *Criminology*, *46*(2), 371–409. https://doi.org/10.1111/j.1745-9125.2008.00113.x.

Goldstein, H. (1979). Improving policing: A problem-oriented approach. *Crime and Delinquency*, *25*(2), 236–258. https://doi.org/10.1177/001112877902500207.

*Goulka, J., Heaton, P., Tita, G., Matthies, C. F., Whitby, A., & Cooper, A. (2009). *FY2006 Anti-Gang Initiative Grants in the Central District of California: Report to the U.S. Attorney*. Santa Monica, CA: RAND Corporation. www.rand.org/pubs/working_papers/WR660.html.

*Green, L. (1996). *Policing Places with Drug Problems*. Drugs, Health and Social Policy Series, vol. 2. Thousand Oaks, CA: Sage Publications.

Griffin, J. W. (2021). Calculating statistical power for meta-analysis using metapower. *Quantitative Methods for Psychology*, *17*(1), 24–39. https://doi.org/10.20982/tqmp.17.1.p024.

Hattingh, H. L., Varsani, J., Kachouei, L. A., & Parsons, R. (2016). Evaluation of pseudoephedrine pharmacy sales before and after mandatory recording requirements in Western Australia: A case study. *Substance Abuse Treatment, Prevention, and Policy*, *11*(1), article 30. https://doi.org/10.1186/s13011-016-0075-0.

Hedges, L. V. (1982). Fitting categorical models to effect sizes from a series of experiments. *Journal of Educational Statistics*, *7*(2), 119–137. https://doi.org/10.3102/10769986007002119.

Hedges, L. V., & Olkin, I. (1985). *Statistical Methods for Meta-analysis*. San Diego, CA: Academic Press.

Hedges, L. V., Tipton, E., & Johnson, M. C. (2010). Robust variance estimation in meta-regression with dependent effect size estimates. *Research Synthesis Methods*, *1*(1), 39–65. https://doi.org/10.1002/jrsm.5.

Higgins, J. P. T., & Thompson, S. G. (2002). Quantifying heterogeneity in a meta-analysis. *Statistics in Medicine*, *21*(11), 1539–1558. https://doi.org/10.1002/sim.1186.

Higgins, J. P. T., López-López, J. A., & Aloe, A. M. (2020). Meta-regression. In C. H. Schmid, T. Stijnen, and I. White (eds.), *Handbook of Meta-analysis* (pp. 129–150). New York: Chapman and Hall/CRC.

Hinkle, J. C., Weisburd, D., Telep, C. W., & Petersen, K. (2020). Problem-oriented policing for reducing crime and disorder: An updated systematic review and meta-analysis. *Campbell Systematic Reviews*, *16*(2), e1089. https://doi.org/10.1002/cl2.1089.

Ho, H., Ko, R., & Mazerolle, L. (2022). Situational crime prevention (SCP) techniques to prevent and control cybercrimes: A focused systematic review. *Computers and Security*, *115*, 102611. https://doi.org/10.1016/j.cose.2022.102611.

*Holder, H. D., Gruenewald, P. J., Ponicki, W. R., Treno, A. J., Grube, J. W., Saltz, R. F., Voas, R. B., Reynolds, R., Davis, J., Sanchez, L., Gaumont, G., & Roeper, P. (2000). Effect of community-based interventions on high-risk drinking and alcohol-related injuries. *Journal of the American Medical Association (JAMA)*, *284*(18), 2341–2347. https://doi.org/10.1001/jama.284.18.2341.

Holmila, M., & Warpenius, K. (2013). Community-based prevention of alcohol-related injuries: Possibilities and experiences. *International Journal of Alcohol and Drug Research*, *1*(1), 27–39. https://doi.org/10.7895/ijadr.v1i1.43.

*Hope, T. (1994). Problem-oriented policing and drug market locations: Three case studies. In R. V. Clarke (ed.), *Crime Prevention Studies*, vol. 2 (pp. 5–32). Monsey, NY: Criminal Justice Press.

Howe, N. (2019). *Policing in Partnership: Are Organic Police Partnerships More Effective Than Mandated Police Partnerships?* PhD thesis, Nottingham Trent University. https://irep.ntu.ac.uk/id/eprint/38009/.

Innes, M., & Roberts, C. (2007). Community intelligence in the policing of community safety. In E. Hogard, R. Ellis, and J. Warren (eds.), *Community Safety: Innovation and Evaluation* (pp. 183–205). Chester: Chester Academic Press.

Johnson, S. D., Tilley, N., & Bowers, K. J. (2015). Introducing EMMIE: An evidence rating scale to encourage mixed-method crime prevention synthesis reviews. *Journal of Experimental Criminology*, *11*(3), 459–473. https://doi.org/10.1007/s11292-015-9238-7.

Kennedy, D. M. (1997). Pulling levers: Chronic offenders, high-crime settings, and a theory of prevention. *Valparaiso University Law Review, 31*(2), 449–484.

*Koehle, G. M. (2011). *An Interrupted Time Series Analysis of the State College Nuisance Property Ordinance and an Assessment of Rental Property Managers as Place Manager/Intimate Handler of Offender.* PhD dissertation, Indiana University of Pennsylvania. www.proquest.com/docview/ 888447044.

*Koper, C. S., Woods, D. J., & Isom, D. (2016). Evaluating a police-led community initiative to reduce gun violence in St. Louis. *Police Quarterly, 19*(2), 115–149. https://doi.org/10.1177/1098611115608506.

Langan, D., Higgins, J. P. T., Jackson, D., Bowden, J., Veroniki, A. A., Kontopantelis, E., Viechtbauer, W., & Simmonds, M. (2019). A comparison of heterogeneity variance estimators in simulated random-effects meta-analyses. *Research Synthesis Methods, 10*(1), 83–98. https://doi.org/10.1002/jrsm.1316.

Lawrence, D. S., La Vigne, N., Jannetta, J., & Fontaine, J. (2019). *Impact of the National Initiative for Building Community Trust and Justice on Police Administrative Outcomes.* Washington, DC: Urban Institute. https://shorturl .at/0V5dz.

Le Ber, M. J., & Branzei, O. (2010). (Re)forming strategic cross-sector partnerships: Relational processes of social innovation. *Business and Society, 49*(1), 140–172. https://doi.org/10.1177/0007650309345457.

Lipsey, M. W., & Wilson, D. B. (2000). *Practical Meta-analysis.* Applied Social Research Methods Series, vol. 49. Thousand Oaks, CA: Sage.

Loader, I. (2000). Plural policing and democratic governance. *Social and Legal Studies, 9*(3), 323–345. https://doi.org/10.1177/096466390000900301.

Lum, C., & Koper, C. S. (2017). *Evidence Based Policing: Translating Research into Practice.* Oxford: Oxford University Press.

Lum, C., Koper, C. S., Wilson, D. B., Stoltz, M., Goodier, M., Eggins, E., Higginson, A., & Mazerolle, L. (2020). Body-worn cameras' effects on police officers and citizen behavior: A systematic review. *Campbell Systematic Reviews, 16*(3), e1112. https://doi.org/10.1002/cl2.1112.

*Lurigio, A. J., Davis, R. C., Regulus, T. A., Gwiasda, V. E., Popkin, S. J., Dantzker, M. L., Smith, B., & Ovellet, L. (1998). *More Effective Place Management: An Evaluation of Cook County's Narcotics Nuisance Abatement Unit.* Crime Prevention Studies, vol. 9: Civil Remedies and Crime Prevention, 9th ed. (pp. 187–218). Monsey, NY: Criminal Justice Press.

Madensen, T. D. (2007). *Bar Management and Crime: Toward a Dynamic Theory of Place Management and Crime Hotspots.* PhD dissertation, University of Cincinnati. http://rave.ohiolink.edu/etdc/view?acc_num=ucin1180461844.

Makin, D. A., & Marenin, O. (2017). Let's dance: Variations of partnerships in community policing. *Policing: A Journal of Policy and Practice*, *11*(4), 421–436. https://doi.org/10.1093/police/paw053.

*Martinez, N. N. (2013). *Team Policing Revisited: A Quasi-experimental Evaluation in Las Vegas, Nevada*. MA thesis, University of Nevada, Las Vegas. http://dx.doi.org/10.34917/4478277.

Mastrofski, S. D., Worden, R. E., & Snipes, J. B. (1995). Law enforcement in a time of community policing. *Criminology*, *33*(4), 539–563. https://doi.org/10.1111/j.1745-9125.1995.tb01189.x.

Matt, G. E. (1989). Decision rules for selecting effect sizes in meta-analysis: A review and reanalysis of psychotherapy outcome studies. *Psychological Bulletin*, *105*(1), 106–115. https://doi.org/10.1037/0033-2909.105.1.106.

Mazerolle, L. (2014). The power of policing partnerships: Sustaining the gains. *Journal of Experimental Criminology*, *10*(3), 341–365. https://doi.org/10.1007/s11292-014-9202-y.

Mazerolle, L., & Ransley, J. (2005). *Third Party Policing*. Cambridge: Cambridge University Press.

Mazerolle, L., & Ransley, J. (2006). The case for third party policing. In D. Weisburd & A. A. Braga (eds.), *Police Innovation: Contrasting Perspectives* (pp. 191–206). Cambridge: Cambridge University Press.

Mazerolle, L., & Ransley, J. (2019). Advocate: Third-party policing. In D. Weisburd & A. A. Braga (eds.), *Police Innovation: Contrasting Perspectives*. Cambridge: Cambridge University Press.

*Mazerolle, L. G., Price, J. F., & Roehl, J. (2000). Civil remedies and drug control: A randomized field trial in Oakland, California. *Evaluation Review*, *24*(2), 212–241. https://doi.org/10.1177/0193841x0002400203.

Mazerolle, L., Ransley, J., Chamlin, M., McGuffog, I., & Ferris, J. (2012). Mandatory reporting of pseudoephedrine sales: An interrupted time series evaluation of Project Stop. *Drug and Alcohol Review*, *31*(S1), 65. https://doi.org/10.1111/j.1465-3362.2012.00514.x.

Mazerolle, L., Eggins, E., & Higginson, A. (2016). PROTOCOL: Third party policing for reducing crime and disorder – A systematic review. *Campbell Systematic Reviews*, *12*(1), 1–77. https://doi.org/10.1002/CL2.153.

Mazerolle, L., McGuffog, I., Ferris, J., & Chamlin, M. B. (2017). Pharmaceutical sales of pseudoephedrine: The impact of electronic tracking systems on methamphetamine crime incidents. *Addiction*, *112*(3), 468–474. https://doi.org/10.1111/add.13648.

*Mazerolle, L., Bennett, S., Antrobus, E., Cardwell, S. M., Eggins, E., & Piquero, A. R. (2019). Disrupting the pathway from truancy to delinquency: A randomized field trial test of the longitudinal impact of a school engagement program. *Journal of Quantitative Criminology*, *35*(4), 663–689. https://doi.org/10.1007/s10940-018-9395-8.

Mazerolle, L., Cherney, A., Eggins, E., Hine, L., & Higginson, A. (2021). Multiagency programs with police as a partner for reducing radicalisation to violence. *Campbell Systematic Reviews*, *17*(2), e1162. https://doi.org/10.1002/cl2.1162.

McAlinden, A.-M. (2006). Managing risk: From regulation to the reintegration of sexual offenders. *Criminology and Criminal Justice*, *6*(2), 197–218. https://doi.org/10.1177/1748895806062981.

Meyer, S., & Mazerolle, L. (2014). Police-led partnership responses to high risk youths and their families: Challenges associated with forming successful and sustainable partnerships. *Policing and Society*, *24*(2), 242–260. https://doi.org/10.1080/10439463.2013.784295.

Millie, A. (2013). The policing task and the expansion (and contraction) of British policing. *Criminology and Criminal Justice*, *13*(2), 143–160. https://doi.org/10.1177/1748895812466393.

Millie, A., & Bullock, K. (2013). Policing in a time of contraction and constraint: Re-imagining the role and function of contemporary policing. *Criminology and Criminal Justice*, *13*(2), 133–142. https://doi.org/10.1177/1748895812474284.

Moreto, W. D., & Gau, J. M. (2017). Deterrence, legitimacy, and Wildlife Crime in Protected Areas. In M. L. Gore (ed.), *Conservation Criminology* (pp. 45–58). Chichester: John Wiley & Sons. https://doi.org/10.1002/9781119376866.ch3.

*Morton, P., Mazerolle, L., Luengen, K., & Newman, M. (2018). Operation Galley: A partnership approach to reducing hotel drug crime. *Police Science*, *3*(1), 7–10.

Morton, P. J., Luengen, K., & Mazerolle, L. (2019). Hoteliers as crime control partners. *Policing: An International Journal of Police Strategies and Management*, *42*(1), 74–88. https://doi.org/10.1108/PIJPSM-08-2018-0126.

Oliver, W. M. (1998). *Community-Oriented Policing: A Systematic Approach to Policing*. Upper Saddle River, NJ: Prentice Hall.

O'Malley, P. (2000). Risk, crime and prudentialism revisited. In K. Stenson & R. Sullivan (eds.), *Risk, Crime and Justice: The Politics of Crime Control in Liberal Democracies* (pp. 89–103). London: Willan.

Ostrom, E., Parks, R. B., Whitaker, G. P., & Percy, S. L. (1978). The public service production process: A framework for analyzing police services. *Policy Studies Journal*, *7*(s1), 381–389. https://doi.org/10.1111/j.1541-0072.1978.tb01782.x.

Ostrom, V., & Ostrom, E. (1979). In E. S. Savas (ed.), *Alternatives for Delivering Public Services: Toward Improved Performance* (pp. 7–49). New York: Routledge.

Pajón, L., & Walsh, D. (2023). The importance of multi-agency collaborations during human trafficking criminal investigations. *Policing and Society, 33* (3), 296–314. https://doi.org/10.1080/10439463.2022.2106984.

*Payne, T. C. (2017). Reducing excessive police incidents: Do notices to owners work? *Security Journal, 30*(3), 922–939. https://doi.org/10.1057/sj.2015.2.

Petersen, K., & Lu, Y.-F. (2023). The downstream effects of body-worn cameras: A systematic review and meta-analysis. *Justice Quarterly, 40*(6), 765–790. https://doi.org/10.1080/07418825.2023.2181855.

Petersen, K., Davis, R. C., Weisburd, D., & Taylor, B. (2022). Effects of second responder programs on repeat incidents of family abuse: An updated systematic review and meta-analysis. *Campbell Systematic Reviews, 18*(1), e1217. https://doi.org/10.1002/cl2.1217.

Petersen, K., Weisburd, D., Fay, S., Eggins, E., & Mazerolle, L. (2023). Police stops to reduce crime: A systematic review and meta-analysis. *Campbell Systematic Reviews, 19*(1), e1302. https://doi.org/10.1002/cl2.1302.

Pires, S., & Clarke, R. V. (2012). Are parrots CRAVED? An analysis of parrot poaching in Mexico. *Journal of Research in Crime and Delinquency, 49*(1), 122–146. https://doi.org/10.1177/0022427810397950.

*Putnam, S. L., Rockett, I. R. H., & Campbell, M. K. (1993). Methodological issues in community-based alcohol-related injury prevention projects: Attribution of program effects. In T. K. Greenfield & R. Zimmerman (eds.), *Experience with Community Action Projects: New Research in the Prevention of Alcohol and Other Drug Problems* (pp. 31–39). Rockville, MD: Center for Substance Abuse Prevention.

Ransley, J. (2016). Policing through third parties: Increasing coercion or improving legitimacy? In M. Deflem (ed.), *The Politics of Policing: Between Force and Legitimacy.* Sociology of Crime, Law and Deviance, vol. 21 (pp. 41–58). Bingley: Emerald.

Ransley, J., & Mazerolle, L. (2009). Policing in an era of uncertainty. *Police Practice and Research, 10*(4), 365–381. https://doi.org/10.1080/15614260802586335.

R Core Team. (2023). R: A language and environment for statistical computing. R Project for Statistical Computing. www.r-project.org/.

Reynald, D. M. (2016). *Guarding Against Crime: Measuring Guardianship within Routine Activity Theory.* Oxfordshire: Routledge.

Rosenthal, R. (1979). The 'file drawer' problem and tolerance for null results. *Psychological Bulletin, 86*(3), 638–641. https://doi.org/10.1037/0033-2909.86.3.638.

Rothstein, H. R. (2008). Publication bias as a threat to the validity of meta-analytic results. *Journal of Experimental Criminology, 4*(1), 61–81. https://doi.org/10.1007/s11292-007-9046-9.

Sampson, R. J. (2010). Gold standard myths: Observations on the experimental turn in quantitative criminology. *Journal of Quantitative Criminology, 26*(4), 489–500. https://doi.org/10.1007/s10940-010-9117-3.

Sampson, R., Eck, J. E., & Dunham, J. (2010). Super controllers and crime prevention: A routine activity explanation of crime prevention success and failure. *Security Journal, 23*(1), 37–51. https://doi.org/10.1057/sj.2009.17.

Sanchez-Meca, J., Marín-Martínez, F., & Chacón-Moscoso, S. (2003). Effect-size indices for dichotomized outcomes in meta-analysis. *Psychological Methods, 8*(4), 448–467. https://doi.org/10.1037/1082-989X.8.4.448.

Scott, C. (2000). Accountability in the regulatory state. *Journal of Law and Society, 27*(1), 38–60. https://doi.org/10.1111/1467-6478.00146.

Scott, M. S. (2018). Effective policing through regulatory control. *Annals of the American Academy of Political and Social Science, 679*(1), 86–104. https://doi.org/10.1177/0002716218778780.

Sedgwick, D., Callahan, J., & Hawdon, J. (2021). Institutionalizing partnerships: A mixed methods approach to identifying trends and perceptions of community policing and multi-agency task forces. *Police Practice and Research, 22*(1), 727–744. https://doi.org/10.1080/15614263.2020.1712204.

Seitanidi, M. M., & Crane, A. (2014). *Social Partnerships and Responsible Business: A Research Handbook.* London: Routledge.

Shadish, W. R., & Heinsman, D. T. (1997). Experiments versus quasi-experiments: Do they yield the same answer? *National Institute on Drug Abuse (NIDA) Research Monograph, 170*, 147–164.

Sherman, L. W. (1998). Evidence-based policing. *Ideas in American Policing Series, July.* Washington, DC: The Police Foundation. https://shorturl.at/m1kr4.

Sherman, L. W., & Weisburd, D. (1995). General deterrent effects of police patrol in crime "hot spots": A randomized, controlled trial. *Justice Quarterly, 12*(4), 625–648. https://doi.org/10.1080/07418829500096221.

Skogan, W. G. (2007). Chicago community policing. In J. R. Greene (ed.), *The Encyclopedia of Police Science,* 3rd ed. (pp. 158–163). New York: Routledge.

Skogan, W. G. (2009). *Police and Community in Chicago: A Tale of Three Cities.* Oxford: Oxford University Press.

Somerville, P. (2009). Understanding community policing. *Policing: An International Journal of Police Strategies and Management, 32*(2), 261–277. https://doi.org/10.1108/13639510910958172.

Stenning, P. C., & Shearing, C. D. (2018). Governing plural policing provision: Legal perspectives, challenges and ideas. In M. den Boer (ed.), *Comparative Policing from a Legal Perspective* (pp. 45–62). Cheltenham: Edward Elgar.

*Sturgeon-Adams, L., Adamson, S., & Davidson, N. (2005). *Hartlepool: A Case Study in Burglary Reduction*. Hull: University of Hull, Centre for Criminology and Criminal Justice. https://popcenter.asu.edu/sites/default/files/177-SturgeonAdams.pdf.

Tanner-Smith, E. E., Tipton, E., & Polanin, J. R. (2016). Handling complex meta-analytic data structures using robust variance estimates: A tutorial in R. *Journal of Developmental and Life-Course Criminology, 2*(1), 85–112. https://doi.org/10.1007/s40865-016-0026-5.

Tantry, T. P., Karanth, H., Shetty, P. K., & Kadam, D. (2021). Self-learning software tools for data analysis in meta-analysis. *Korean Journal of Anesthesiology, 74* (5), 459–461. https://doi.org/10.4097/KJA.21080.

Telep, C. W., Weisburd, D., Gill, C. E., Vitter, Z., & Teichman, D. (2014). Displacement of crime and diffusion of crime control benefits in large-scale geographic areas: A systematic review. *Journal of Experimental Criminology, 10*(4), 515–548. https://doi.org/10.1007/s11292-014-9208-5.

Thacher, D. (2022). Shrinking the police footprint. *Criminal Justice Ethics, 41* (1), 62–85. https://doi.org/10.1080/0731129X.2022.2062546.

Tillyer, M. S., & Eck, J. E. (2011). Getting a handle on crime: A further extension of routine activities theory. *Security Journal, 24*(2), 179–193. https://doi.org/10.1057/sj.2010.2.

*Tita, G., Riley, K. J., Ridgeway, G., Grammich, C. A., Abrahamse, A., & Greenwood, P. W. (2011). *Reducing Gun Violence: Results from an Intervention in East Los Angeles*. Santa Monica, CA: RAND Corporation. https://doi.org/10.7249/MR1764-1.

Topping, J. (2022). Austerity, path dependency and the (re)configuration of policing. *Policing and Society, 32*(6), 715–730. https://doi.org/10.1080/10439463.2021.1965142.

van Felius, M., Bates, L., Ransley, J., & Martin, P. (2023). Engaging non-policing partners to prevent or respond to crime. *Policing and Society, 33*(6), 717–731. https://doi.org/10.1080/10439463.2023.2189251.

van Tulder, R., & Keen, N. (2018). Capturing collaborative challenges: Designing complexity-sensitive theories of change for cross-sector partnerships. *Journal of Business Ethics, 150*(2), 315–332. https://doi.org/10.1007/s10551-018-3857-7.

van Tulder, R., Seitanidi, M. M., Crane, A., & Brammer, S. (2016). Enhancing the impact of cross-sector partnerships. *Journal of Business Ethics*, *135*(1), 1–17. https://doi.org/10.1007/s10551-015-2756-4.

Viechtbauer, W. (2010). Conducting meta-analyses in R with the metafor package. *Journal of Statistical Software*, *36*(3), 1–48. https://doi.org/10.18637/jss.v036.i03.

*Warpenius, K., & Holmila, M. (2008). Local prevention in licensed premises: Experiences from the Finnish PAKKA project. In B. Olssson & J. Törrönen (eds.), *Painting the Town Red: Pubs', Restaurants' and Young Adults' Drinking Cultures in the Nordic Countries*. NAD Publication No. 51 (pp. 249–272). Helsinki: Nordic Centre for Alcohol and Drug Research (NAD).

Warpenius, K., Holmila, M., & Mustonen, H. (2010). Effects of a community intervention to reduce the serving of alcohol to intoxicated patrons. *Addiction*, *105*(6), 1032–1040. https://doi.org/10.1111/j.1360-0443.2009.02873.x.

Webster, J., Mazerolle, P., Ransley, J., & Mazerolle, L. (2017). Disrupting domestic "ice" production: Deterring drug runners with a third-party policing intervention. *Policing and Society*, *28*(9), 1025–1037. https://doi.org/10.1080/10439463.2016.1272602.

Weisburd, D. (2015). The law of crime concentration and the criminology of place. *Criminology*, *53*(2), 133–157. https://doi.org/10.1111/1745-9125.12070.

Weisburd, D., & Braga, A. A. (eds.) (2019). *Police Innovation: Contrasting Perspectives*, 2nd ed. Cambridge: Cambridge University Press. https://doi.org/10.1017/9781108278423.

Weisburd, D., & Eck, J. E. (2004). What can police do to reduce crime, disorder, and fear? *Annals of the American Academy of Political and Social Science*, *593*(1), 42–65. https://doi.org/10.1177/0002716203262548.

Weisburd, D., & Majmundar, M. K. (2018). *Proactive policing: Effects on crime and communities*. Washington, DC: National Academies of Sciences.

Weisburd, D., Lum, C. M., & Petrosino, A. (2001). Does research design affect study outcomes in criminal justice? *Annals of the American Academy of Political and Social Science*, *578*(1), 50–70. https://doi.org/10.1177/000271620157800104.

Weisburd, D., Wyckoff, L. A., Ready, J., Eck, J. E., Hinkle, J. C., & Gajewski, F. (2006). Does crime just move around the corner? A controlled study of spatial displacement and diffusion of crime control benefits. *Criminology*, *44*(3), 549–592. https://doi.org/10.1111/j.1745-9125.2006.00057.x.

Weisburd, D., Gill, C., Wooditch, A., Barritt, W., & Murphy, J. (2021). Building collective action at crime hot spots: Findings from a randomized field experiment. *Journal of Experimental Criminology*, *17*(2), 161–191. https://doi.org/10.1007/s11292-019-09401-1.

Weisburd, D., Wilson, D. B., Wooditch, A., & Britt, C. L. (2022). *Advanced Statistics in Criminology and Criminal Justice*, 5th ed. Cham: Springer.

Welsh, B. C., & Farrington, D. P. (2008). Effects of closed circuit television surveillance on crime. *Campbell Systematic Review*, *4*(1), 1–73. https://doi.org/10.4073/csr.2008.17.

*White, M., Fyfe, J., Campbell, S., & Goldkamp, J. (2003). The police role in preventing homicide: Considering the impact of problem-oriented policing on the prevalence of murder. *Journal of Research in Crime and Delinquency*, *40*(2), 194–225. https://doi.org/10.1177/0022427803251126.

Wilson, D. B. (2022). The relative incident rate ratio effect size for count-based impact evaluations: When an odds ratio is not an odds ratio. *Journal of Quantitative Criminology*, *38*(2), 323–341. https://doi.org/10.1007/s10940-021-09494-w.

Wilson, D. B., Feder, L., & Olaghere, A. (2021). Court-mandated interventions for individuals convicted of domestic violence: An updated Campbell systematic review. *Campbell Systematic Reviews*, *17*(1), e1151. https://doi.org/10.1002/cl2.1151.

Wood, J., & Shearing, C. (2006). *Imagining Security*. London: Willan.

Zahnow, R., & Corcoran, J. (2022). Living near violence and feeling safe: What is the role of active guardianship in the home territory? *Journal of Quantitative Criminology*, *38*(1), 105–126. https://doi.org/10.1007/s10940-020-09486-2.

Zedner, L., & Ashworth, A. (2019). The rise and restraint of the preventive state. *Annual Review of Criminology*, *2*, 429–450. https://doi.org/10.1146/annurev-criminol-011518-024526.

Cambridge Elements ☰

Criminology

David Weisburd
George Mason University, Virginia
Hebrew University of Jerusalem

Advisory Board

About the Series

Elements in Criminology seeks to identify key contributions in theory and empirical research that help to identify, enable, and stake out advances in contemporary criminology. The series focuses on radical new ways of understanding and framing criminology, whether of place, communities, persons, or situations. The relevance of criminology for preventing and controlling crime is also be a key focus of this series.

Cambridge Elements ≡

Criminology

Elements in the Series

Printed in the United States
by Baker & Taylor Publisher Services